A HISTORY OF HAMPSHIRE

WITH MAPS AND PICTURES

by

BARBARA CARPENTER TURNER

Cartography by H. S. PARSONS

DARWEN FINLAYSON BEACONSFIELD, ENGLAND

First published 1963
Re-issued 1969

DARWEN FINLAYSON LIMITED
CRENDON HOUSE, STATION ROAD, BEACONSFIELD, BUCKS
PRINTED IN GREAT BRITAIN BY COX & WYMAN LTD
LONDON, FAKENHAM AND READING

CONTENTS

MAPS AND PLANS

LIST OF ILLUSTRATIONS

The illustration numbered 3 is reproduced by kind permission from The Duke of Wellington's collection at Reading Museum; numbers 2, 4, 5, 6, and 12 by courtesy of the British Museum; numbers 1, 8, 9, by courtesy of Aerofilms, Ltd.; number 7 by courtesy of the Society of Antiquaries of London; number 10 by courtesy of E. A. Sollars, Esq.; number 13 by courtesy of the National Trust from a photograph by A. F. Kersting; number 14 by courtesy of the Hampshire Field Club and Archaeological Society; number 15 by courtesy of Portals, Ltd., and is a photograph by M.C. Fleet; number 16 by courtesy of Sir Anthony Tichborne, Bt., and from a print supplied by the Royal Academy of Arts; numbers 18 and 21 by courtesy of the Bournemouth Public Libraries; numbers 19 and 22 by courtesy of the National Portrait Gallery; number 20 from the miniature by John Hoskins in the National Museum, Stockholm; number 24 by courtesy of the Friends of Portsmouth Cathedral; and number 25 by courtesy of the *Southern Evening Echo*. The map of Roman Hampshire on page 11 is reproduced from the Ordinance Survey Map with the sanction of the Controller of H. M. Stationery Office. Crown Copyright reserved. The map of Calleva on page 13 is reproduced by permission of Reading Museum and Art Gallery; and the plans of The Vyne on pages 46 and 47 are reproduced from *The History of The Vyne* by Challoner Chute, by kind permission of Miss Chute.

PREFACE

The writing of this book would not have been possible if it had not been the author's privilege to have the most generous help from many people. I want to take this opportunity of recording here the debt I owe to the hundreds of people, not all of them academics by any means, but with whom I have had the opportunity of discussing local history in the last twenty-five years. Some have been patient individuals in lecture groups; others I know only as correspondents; many have been members of our county antiquarian society, the Hampshire Field Club, or of the Historical Association in Hampshire, or of one of the many local societies deeply concerned with local history. I should like to thank them all, especially those who are not professional historians, for their enthusiasm and encouragement; it would be a sad day indeed for Hampshire were the county's history to be of interest only to a handful of qualified technicians.

I want to record also my grateful thanks for the courteous and efficient help given me by the staff of the Hampshire County Record Office ever since it opened in 1947; the help I have had from Curators of Museums at Alton, Portsmouth, Southampton, Reading and Winchester; the help I have had from Public Libraries throughout the county, and in particular from the Borough Librarian at Bournemouth, and from two successive City Librarians at Winchester. Moreover, no historian can live in a vacuum, and I owe more than I can say to those individuals who have so generously shared with me their knowledge of different Hampshire localities or subjects; in particular I am indebted to the Rev. S. E. Hockey, Dr. Alwyn Ruddock, Miss Elsie Sandell, Mr. John Harvey, Mr. F. Emery Wallis, Mr. Victor Bonham-Carter, and Mr. D. G. Watts. I should like to thank the Editor of the *Hampshire Chronicle*, Mrs. Woodhouse, for kindly allowing me to make use of the files of her long established county newspaper; Mr. G. Gardner, the Bishop's Registrar, and Mr. A. G. Willis, for their help with diocesan records; I want to thank the Dean and Chapter of Winchester Cathedral and their Librarian, the Rev. Canon J. P. Boden, not only for allowing me to consult their archives but for the privilege of being able to work in the peace of the Cathedral Library. To the Cathedral's Deputy Librarian, Miss Beatrice Forder, I am particularly grateful, and I must record here the debt which all historians of our county—present and future—owe her for the scrupulous care and skill with which she has repaired or is repairing the documents and books of our great county archive collections, at the Winchester City Record Office, at the Hampshire County Office, and in the Cathedral Library. I have been much helped by the skill of my cartographer, Mr. H. S. Parsons, and by the efficiency of Mrs. J. H. Preston who typed my manuscript.

In the making of this book I have been fortunate in my publisher. It has been a great privilege to work with Lord Darwen, and to have the benefit of his wisdom and knowledge as a publisher of local history.

INTRODUCTION

The county of Hampshire may rightly claim an honourable place in English history. Its strategic and vital position in the centre of southern England, its proximity to the Continent, and to London, the fact that for many years its county town and cathedral city, Winchester, was also the national capital have all been factors which have helped to make the history of Hampshire also in part the history of England.

Hampshire's story has been much influenced by her sea coast, but this coast was not formed, even incompletely, until six or seven thousand years before the birth of Christ when the Isle of Wight was cut away by the great Solent river system. This important change appears to have been the result of a milder climate, much melting of ice, and a rise in sea level, all of which eventually led to a separation of Britain from the Continent. A number of excellent natural harbours have always encouraged trade and commerce, and in later years the growth of the Royal Navy has been an important influence on Portsmouth and its hinterland. The English Channel, though a vital defence in times of war, does more than divide Hampshire from the Continent; in the early days of Hampshire history it was an important means of communication, bringing to the county new products of trade and industry, new ideas, and new peoples.

Inland, the rivers and the chalk downs have affected the course of the county's history. The Meon, the Itchen, the Test, and the Hampshire Avon were all rivers which made the county accessible to primitive peoples, though they could also be used as defence lines. The great chalk downs in primeval times were covered with yew and other indigenous vegetation, but when the climate became warmer and drier (roughly 2500–2000 B. C.) and primitive farmers began to clear the downs, yew trees gave way to that most characteristic of all features of the Hampshire countryside, the downland turf grazed by cattle and later by sheep. Though there were periods when large areas of downland were under plough for grain crops, much of the county's prosperity has been founded on sheep-farming and the woollen industry. There are indeed those who would maintain that that curious county animal the 'Hampshire Hog' is not really a pig, as it is on the weather-vane of the new headquarters of the County Council in Winchester, but a hoggett, that is a sheep. It must be said that there have always been plenty of pigs in Hampshire, particularly in the south-west, in the New Forest, which may or may not have been created by order of William the Conqueror, but which is certainly a part of the county which maintains a particular character and charm of its own.

The county town, Winchester, has been for generations also the cathedral city of the great diocese of Winchester. The diocese and many of its bishops often played an important part in the county's history. Yet Hampshire apparently derives its name from its great port, Southampton; it is the shire of Hampton, and until 1st April, 1959, the official designation of the administrative county was the county of Southampton. It is now once more Hampshire, as it was to the compilers of the *Anglo-Saxon Chronicle* at the very beginning of its history as a separate administrative unit. For Hampshire, at vital periods in the past, before it was a shire, was sometimes included in wider divisions of southern England: it was part of the Celtic kingdom of the Atrebates, of the Roman canton of the Belgae: it is still part of historic Wessex.

Today Hampshire is affected by population pressure and movements as it was over two thousand years ago. New problems have been created by industrial development on the coast; small Hampshire inland towns are to be expanded as 'overspill' centres, with thousands of new residents from over-large London. Hundreds of people settle in the county each year because, as holiday makers, they have already learned to love its differing beauties. This is all perhaps as it should be, but it is to be hoped that Hampshire will retain the quiet beauty of her villages and countryside, as well as the essential and differing vitalities of her larger towns and her coastline as an unbroken and undissipated inheritance, safe in the keeping of each new generation.

I

Hampshire before the Roman Occupation

THE first human inhabitants of Hampshire of whom anything is known were brutish hunters, many of whom lived along the river valleys, existing on what they could kill, and making no attempt to farm the land. The climate was damp and cold, and the downs were heavily forested with yew, and difficult of access. The Isle of Wight was part of the mainland, till the waters of the English Channel flowed into the great Solent river system, and cut the Island away, probably destroying much evidence of the life and culture of mesolithic Hampshire man, of whom it is certain that flint was his essential material. From flint he made his weapons and primitive tools, objects manufactured in enormous quantities on certain easily recognized inland sites, at Old Winchester Hill, at Beaulieu and in the New Forest, some sites near large ponds supplying water-fowl and fish for the makers of flint weapons. At Oakhammer Pond, near Selborne, some three thousand flint implements were recently recorded. Flint, so long a traditional and local building material in Hampshire was thus the raw material which provided the county's first industry.

In comparison with the people who came after them, these early flint users have left little trace on the Hampshire countryside. Their successors, the peoples of later prehistory, a long period of years before the Roman Conquest of A.D. 43, have left behind much visible and enduring evidence as to their communities, their way of life and particularly their way of burial after death. All over Hampshire can still be seen the great hill forts, the groups of *tumuli*, the barrows of many kinds, the ancient tracks and primitive fields which provide a variety of evidence for the field archaeologist and the excavator.

Later, about two thousand years before Christ, primitive farmers arrived in Hampshire, who knew how to hoe the land and to domesticate and graze animals. They could make primitive pottery, and wore garments of cowhide, for they could not weave. Some, perhaps were cannibals. The clearance of the chalk downs began. In the districts bordering on Hampshire these neolithic people built causeway camps (for example, on Windmill Hill, Wiltshire, and on The Trundle, Sussex), where an autumn poleaxing of cattle took place. They buried their dead carefully in communal graves for both sexes, carefully constructed long barrows like those at Danebury, Moody's Down, Chilbolton Down, and Bevis' Grave (now destroyed) at Portsdown.

In about 1800 B.C., a new invader came to southern England. These Beaker folk, so-called because of the shape of their pottery, buried their dead individually in round barrows. Unlike their predecessors they grew little wheat; their main crop was barley. They still used flints, but had some objects of metal. A girl buried at the top of Stockbridge Down had a small bronze awl in her grave, as well as a beaker. The gradual disappearance of the Beaker folk, or their integration with other cultures marks the beginning of the Bronze Age when metal objects came into general use.

Bronze was the metal of the rich and various objects which tell so much about these new invaders, their wide trading contacts with the Continent, their warrior aristocracy. Their chief port appears to have been at Hengistbury Head; here have been found ornaments of bronze and amber which may imply trade with the eastern Mediterranean. In the Middle Bronze Age cremation became the usual form of burial; in this and in the Early Bronze period individuals were buried in round barrows of various types of which many can still be seen on or near the ancient ridgeways across the Downs. The Seven

Barrows of Burghclere are unusually placed, in a valley, the great group of Popham Beacons form a delightful part of a high downland landscape. There are others on Butser and in the Isle of Wight, where the ancient ridgeway from the Needles has at least twelve barrows scattered on it. Barrows are of distinctive types, bell, disc, saucer, and pond; the great bell-barrow at Bishop's Waltham was probably the burial place of some Bronze Age chieftain.

In about 1000 B.C. new invaders came to Hampshire, Deverel-Rimbury people, called after two of their burial places in Dorset. They left behind many scattered burials in Hampshire, particularly in the Christchurch region, and one of their farms has been excavated at Thorny Down near Boscombe Down East. They herded their cattle in large ranches and enclosures. Two bronze twisted torques found at Plaitford and many other finds on the borders of Hampshire show that they were not just peasant farmers, but wealthy men able to buy goods of quality and of distant origin. A trader's hoard of axes, found at Nether Wallop, are of a type originating in Brittany. It was indeed from north-western France that the next wave of invaders came to Hampshire, urged there perhaps by a need of land and by tribal unrest. Again, their landing-place in the county may have been Hengistbury Head. They were Celtic-speaking users of tools and weapons of iron, practising new and improved methods of farming. Unlike their predecessors, they were practically self-sufficient and widespread trade was not a feature of their economy. They grew large quantities of barley, storing the grain in carefully prepared pits and granaries. As yet nothing is really known of their farm buildings in Hampshire, but these Iron Age farmers, whom archaeologists divide into three successive chronological groups, Iron Age A, B and C, have left some really notable marks on the countryside for they were the makers of the great hill forts, constructed and reconstructed at different times but intended as places of refuge and

defence against further invasion threats from the Continent. Amongst the defences thus constructed in about 250 B.C. are the simple hill forts of Quarley and Ladle Hill, the latter particularly interesting because the wave of invasion apparently died away and the fortification was unfinished. Julius Caesar's defeat of the Venetii of Brittany nearly two hundred years later meant that many refugees came to Hampshire and Dorset, some of them landing at Hengistbury Head. The year 56 B.C., therefore, has been called a turning-point in the fortunes of Wessex, and many of these people, whose characteristic weapon was the sling, eventually found refuge in the great fortress of Maiden Castle. Thousands of sling stones were recently found in the defences there, for Maiden became the great tribal headquarters of the refugee Gauls who became known in Wessex as Durotriges, controlling not only Dorset but also the western borders of Hampshire. Some of their primitive coins were minted at Hengistbury, and it has been suggested, on coin evidence, that their boundary on the east was the Hampshire Avon.

The greater part of Hampshire, however, was eventually possessed by refugees from Caesar's government in Northern Gaul, and though the native inhabitants appear to have tried to secure the county by the re-fortification of some hill forts, notably those along the Test valley at Danebury and Bury Hill, it was an effort made in vain.

In the south-east of the county, the refugee leader of the Gaulish Atrebates, King Commius, whose first settlement was probably at Selsey, penetrated into Hampshire, and may or may not have been able to get as far north as Silchester before he died in 20 B.C. His son or grandson, Eppillus, was the first British ruler to use the word Rex on his coins. Silchester, known to the Romans as *Calleva Atrebatum* seems to have been the capital of the Atrebates in Hampshire, but most of their land was eventually conquered by the Catuvellauni of King Cunobelinus (Cymbeline) whose capital was Colchester

(*Camulodunum*), and whose son Caractacus was too powerful an influence to be left undisturbed by the Roman Emperor Claudius. The civilization which the Romans found in Hampshire can conveniently be called Celtic, but it was a combination of various elements, and there was no uniform pattern. In the greater part of the county, the dominating influence was that of the later refugee tribes, the Atrebatic and Catuvellaunian peoples whose culture is so often called Belgic, but who controlled many peasants and simple farmers of older non-Belgic Iron Age stock. Political power was in the hands of the warriors and the Druid priests. It would be a mistake to suggest that the Belgae in Hampshire had a culture which surpassed that of their Roman conquerors, but Celtic civilization did in fact reach a high standard. Belgic invaders brought with them a new type of plough with which they were able to cultivate difficult and heavy land not previously used for grain production. They were thus able to grow vast quantities of cereals which they stored in pits and in large jars; traces of Celtic fields, small and square,

survive in many parts of the county. Though even recent excavation has revealed little evidence as to the nature of possible Belgic 'towns' in Hampshire, it seems reasonably certain that the hill forts used and re-used by earlier peoples as places of refuge were not their centres. *Venta Belgarum* may have been one of their marketing towns, as its later Roman name certainly would suggest, but it was not important enough to have a mint. The primitive coinage of Celtic Wessex, a coinage of silver and gold, implies not only trade, and wealthy sections of the community able to purchase luxury goods, but also a desire to imitate that Roman civilization which was soon to impose its uniformity all over England.

Further Reading: Essays in Honour of Frank Warren: Hampshire in the British Iron Age, C. F. C. Hawkes (H.F.C., Vol. XX, 1956).
The Archaeology of Wessex, L. V. Grinsell (Methuen, 1958).
Wessex Before the Celts, J. F. S. Stone (Thames and Hudson, 1958).
Wessex from the Air, O. G. S. Crawford and A. Keiller (Clarendon Press, 1928).
Field Archaeology as illustrated by Hampshire, J. P. Williams-Freeman, 1915.

II

Roman Hampshire

THE real conquest of Britain began in A.D. 43 on the order of the Emperor Claudius. One of the reasons for his decision was the appeal of the last of the Atrebate princes of Hampshire, Verica, against Caractacus, and the violence of 'Cymbeline's' other successors. Southern England could have become a dangerous centre of resistance to Roman rule, and at this point Claudius ordered the conquest of Britain, for she was too independent and her wealth made her a desirable addition to the Roman Empire. The military subjection of Hampshire was part of the successful campaign of the Roman general Vespasian (the later Emperor) in command of the Second Legion. The capture of Maiden Castle, near Dorchester, was a climax in his campaign, and perhaps implies the subjection of Hampshire. It was certainly accompanied or followed by the annexation of the Isle of Wight. There is no evidence to suggest that the native inhabitants either in the mainland or on the island offered much resistance. Caractacus was betrayed to the Romans by the queen of a rival tribe.

Unlike great areas in the north of Britain, the Roman occupation of Hampshire was not primarily of a military nature. Roman local government areas or cantons only partially coincided with the old Celtic tribal boundaries. The power of the Atrebates was not revived and only a small section of the north of the county was included in their canton. This included the capital *Calleva Atrebatum* but the Roman town there did not coincide entirely with the older settlement of Silchester. The rest of the coast, including apparently the Isle of Wight, formed a large part of the canton of the Belgae. This canton stretched far to the west, where its chief town was *Aquae Sulis* (Bath), but the eastern, Hampshire sector, included the cantonal capital *Venta Belgarum* (Winchester). In this sector were a number of other important Roman settlements, a port of *Clausentum* (Bitterne, near Southampton) and road stations at *Vindomis* (unidentified, between Silchester and Winchester), and *Brige*, thought perhaps to be the small market town of Stockbridge. The canton of the Belgae, a large area, appears to have been an artificial creation of the Romans who also left some important tribal centres to decline, for example Hengistbury Head where there had been a mint of the Durotriges.

A predominantly British population continued to work the land and to live in the towns, with the addition of some 'Roman' landlords, many government officials, and some retired soldiers, as well as the garrison troops. The land was worked from a number of farmsteads. Certain 'villas' were apparently official centres of large government farming enterprises. There are large stock enclosures at Rockbourne and Damerham, and that great authority on Roman Britain, R. G. Collingwood, believed that the existence of a government weaving mill at *Venta Belgarum*, making cloth for the army, indicated widespread official sheep-farming on the Hampshire downs, replacing the corn grown in Celtic times.

Other villas were just pleasant and smaller country houses for wealthy Romano-British gentlemen. There were a number of these small villas in the Isle of Wight, though the most famous villa there is the large composite group at Brading, including a bath block and domestic buildings with very fine mosaic pavements. On the mainland the important villa at Rockbourne, near Fordingbridge, has only recently been partially excavated. It stands in the midst of good farming land, was perhaps an important stock centre, and was lived in, though not continuously, until

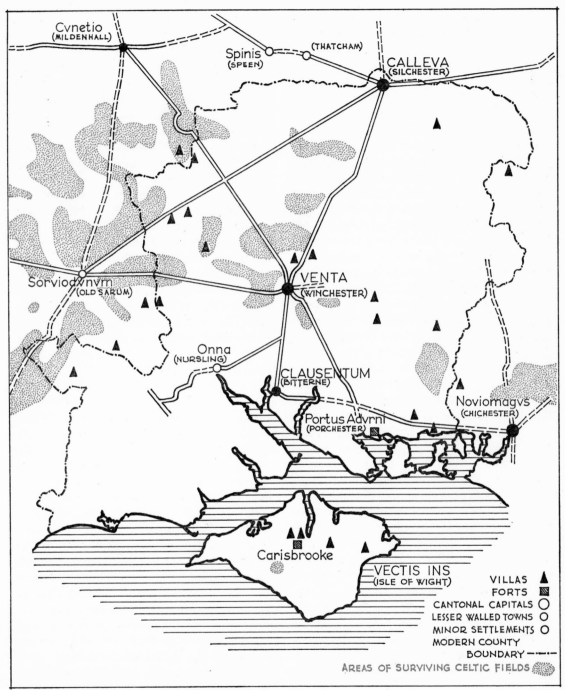

Map 1. Roman Hampshire

the end of the Roman occupation. Its many rooms include a 'red room' with a floor of tesserae in swastika pattern, and walls decorated with Pompeian red plaster and a grey and black dado. Many other villas cluster round Andover and Winchester. West Wood (Sparsholt), Grateley, Fullerton, Longstock and Abbott's Ann, have all been excavated and belong to the later years of the occupation. To the fourth century A.D. also belongs Lodge Farm, near North Warnborough, an earlier homestead, not on the direct line of any known Roman highway, which was turned into the bath-house of a simple 'villa' perhaps occupied by farm servants or other humble Romano-British folk. It was large, but its wattle partitions and chalk floors suggest that it was occupied by farm hands or domestic staff. These houses were probably in private ownership. Of course not all the owners were 'Roman', some were Romanized Britons. The Romanization of British life began when Agricola was governor of Britain (A.D. 77–84), perhaps with government backing, though the majority of the native inhabitants continued to live squalidly and simply in huts. Some made use of the new and improved type of pottery produced by many Roman kilns in the New Forest. The villagers of Stockbridge Down possessed a few luxuries such as imitation Samian bowls. Though the conquerors brought a new coinage (there was perhaps a mint at *Clausentum*) Celtic coins continued to be the currency of the more backward part of the county.

A greatly improved road system was a more obvious and material result of the coming of the Romans. The roads probably date from the early years of the occupation; military need rather than trade was the reason for their construction. *Venta Belgarum* (Winchester) was an important focal point in the system. How far, if at all, the city had been developed as a Belgic market town before the invasion is as yet impossible to say though there is much evidence of pre-Roman habitation around it, on St. Catherine's Hill, on Hockley Down, and on the western down of St. Paul's Hill. The site of *Venta* is still a flourishing and occupied part of modern Winchester, and excavation has therefore been only of a limited nature. Enough has been done to show that there were large and important buildings in the centre of the city and that part of the city wall is Roman in origin. The site of the government weaving mill has not yet been discovered.

In contrast to Winchester, *Calleva Atrebatum* (Silchester) is the only Roman town in England to be fully excavated. The whole of *Calleva* was laid out on a grid system of roads whose sides were crowded with shops, houses and administrative offices. There can be no doubt that this town played an important part in the Romanization of northern Hampshire. Some of its bricks bear an official Neronian stamp. Recent re-excavation has confirmed the existence at *Calleva* of England's only Christian church of the Roman occupation, a building small in size when compared with the town's pagan temples, forum, public baths and rest house for the Imperial post.

In the later years of the Roman occupation, when Saxon pirates were already active, Roman settlements and ports on the Hampshire coast played their part as defences against the invaders. The great fortification of Portchester still remains, with its walls and bastions. A shore-port at Carisbrooke helped to defend the Isle of Wight. The port of *Clausentum* was at first fortified by a simple wooden stockade across its peninsula (A.D. 120–150). A late stone wall suggests that its defences were reconstructed by order of Count Theodosius, Civil Governor of Britain in A.D. 368. Yet despite the potential strength of the coastal fortifications once the decision was taken to withdraw the Roman army, the fate of Hampshire and of Britain was settled. A new era of history began with the *Adventus Saxonum*, the coming of the Saxons.

Tradition and archaeology both suggest that Christianity first reached Hampshire in

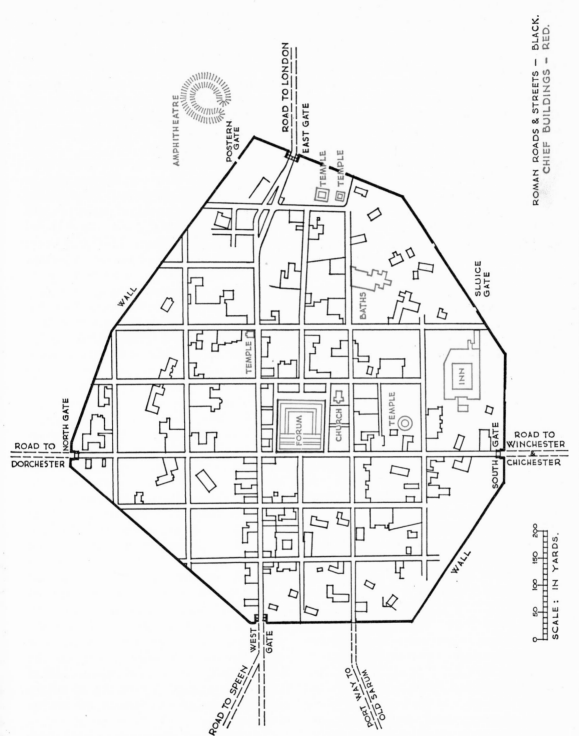

ROMAN ROADS & STREETS — BLACK.
CHIEF BUILDINGS — RED.

Map 2.   *Simplified Plan of CALLEVA ATREBATUM (Silchester).*

the Roman period. It is probable that the faith came with the traders who crossed the Channel in the wake of the army rather than with the army itself, where empire worship and the cult of Mithras were formidable rivals to Christianity. British bishops were present at the Council of Arles in 315, and about a hundred years later the Pelagian heresy was rife in southern England, a heresy combated by the preaching of St. Germanus of Auxerre who is said to have landed on the Hampshire coast between Portsmouth and Southampton and healed the son of the leading man of the region, a tradition which suggests that Christianity, for a short while at least, survived the withdrawal of the Roman army. A gold ring found at Silchester in 1786 inscribed with a common Christian formula, a small lead seal or stamp with a Christian monogram (formed from the Greek letters Chi and Rho) from the same town, and the small Christian church near *Calleva's* 'forum' are the only archaeological traces of Christianity in Roman Hampshire.

When the conversion of Hampshire began again in the seventh century, the inhabitants were said to be heathen. This disappearance of Christianity was perhaps significant; Romano-British civilization did not prove to be a permanent foundation for the future development of Hampshire.

Further reading: Town and County in Roman Britain, A. L. F. Rivet (Hutchinson, 1958).
Roman Britain, I. A. Richmond (Pelican History of England, 1955).
The Roman Villa at Rockbourne, Hampshire, A. T. Morley-Hewitt (Bennet, Salisbury, 1960).
'The Roman House at Lodge Farm', D. M. Liddell (H.F.C. *Proceedings*, Vol. X, 1931).
Excavations at Clausentum, 1951–54, M. Alwyn Cotton, and P. W. Gathercole (H.M. Stationery Office, 1958).
Roman Silchester, G. C. Boon (Parrish, 1957).
'The Lost Settlement of Brige', R. Hill. (H.F.C. *Proceedings*, Vol. XX, 1956).

III

The Coming of the Saxons and the Conversion of Hampshire to Christianity

IN the second half of the third century southern England was again troubled by invaders from across the sea. The English historian Bede, whose *History of the English Church and People* was completed in A.D. 731 calls these invaders Angles, Saxons and Jutes. Though Bede was a northerner, writing at Jarrow, he took great care to make his account of what happened in the south as accurate as possible and specifically says that he consulted his friend Daniel, Bishop of Winchester from 705 until 744, about the early history of the diocese.

The new invaders were of Germanic origin, and can be conveniently referred to here as Saxons for though the Angles gave their name to the country as a whole, certain Saxon groups established themselves in parts of England henceforth called after them, amongst them the West-Saxons of Wessex, which includes Hampshire, though much of the present county, parts of the New Forest and the Isle of Wight were settled by Jutes. Because of these invasions the Romans called the south-east coast of England the Saxon Shore. They were forced to increase its garrisons and its fortifications, and special sea patrols reported the movement of pirate vessels. Yet the invaders continued their raids, and when invasions by barbarians in other parts of the Roman Empire forced the Romans to withdraw their troops from England a period of confusion and uncertainty followed. The most reliable accounts of what happened in England when the Romans left are to be found in Bede and in the great *Anglo-Saxon Chronicle* but neither Bede nor those who wrote down the traditions of their forefathers in the *Chronicle* were contemporary with the events they describe and the writers of the *Chronicle* were perhaps anxious to please the kings whose Saxon ancestors had carried out the conquest of England. According to the *Chronicle*, the conquest of Hampshire began in A.D. 495, when a Saxon warrior chief Cerdic and his son, Cynric (probably really his grandson) landed from a small fleet of ships at Cerdicesora, a place which was probably somewhere on the New Forest side of Southampton Water. Cerdic was the ancestor of the royal house of Wessex, whose activities form an important part of the *Chronicle*. By A.D. 530 he and his followers had conquered the Isle of Wight which he is said to have given to his 'kinsmen', Stuf and Whitgar in 534, the year in which he died.

Archaeological evidence suggests that the Jutes were prominent in the settlement of both the mainland and of the Island. At Chessel Down in the Island, excavations carried out between 1816 and 1855 recovered more than a hundred and thirty Jutish graves, amongst them that of a warrior chieftain whose body had been prepared for burial with a veil or band, decorated with gold thread, covering his forehead; an iron girdle; silver gilt brooches; near his hand a dark wine-coloured crystal ball, probably contained in a silver gilt spoon. An earlier landing, at Portsmouth, was also probably Jutish. The *Chronicle* records that in 501, Port and his sons Bieda and Maegla came there with two ships and killed a British nobleman. The Jutes, too, conquered the valley of the River Meon; at Droxford, a large Jutish cemetery has produced grave goods of various kinds, swords, spearheads, shields and bosses. In eastern Hampshire the invaders were clearly able to make good use of the Meon River, following its valley inland, as Saxon bands followed the valley of the Test and of the Itchen. The invaders' movements towards the west may have been halted in about A.D. 552 by a British stand at what is now Old Sarum, but there appears to have been little organized opposition to the bands of invading Saxon raiders. The conquest of Hampshire was piecemeal and those Britons who tried to resist were either killed, captured as slaves, or driven farther westwards to the eventual isolation of Wales and of Cornwall. Romano-British civilization could offer little that was acceptable to the rough and illiterate warrior bands, and though there were skilled craftsmen amongst them, in general the Saxon invaders either destroyed or avoided the villas and towns of Roman Hampshire and *Calleva* was deserted.

When the initial period of conquest came to an end, the Saxons settled in new villages which had grown up along the river valleys and a trading settlement began to develop at the mouth of the Itchen. The revival of town life did not occur, however, until the later Saxon period, and the main peacetime occupation of early Hampshire Anglo-Saxons was farming, the growing of barley for food and drink, and the slow clearance of forest land, though the area of the New Forest remained virtually uninhabited. The usual distinctions of society divided men into those of noble birth and those who worked on the land as freemen, ceorls, or as serfs. What happened to *Venta Belgarum* is not yet known, but town life eventually did begin to redevelop amongst the ruins of Roman Winchester, if indeed the continuity was ever completely broken. Pagan Saxon cemeteries in the neighbourhood include those at Abbot's Worthy, Micheldever, and St. Giles' Hill. St. Giles' Hill dominates Winchester, and the pagan Saxons buried there with their iron spear-heads, knives, swords and shields must have constituted when alive a very real threat to the Roman city lying below. A delicate silver ring found on the same hill can be regarded as a most hopeful token for a civilized future. Not far away, at Oliver's Battery, a splendid hanging bowl in a burial

pushed into a Romano-British earthwork (which takes its name from the time when Cromwell's soldiers were there in 1645) provides magnificent evidence of a high standard of pagan art and craftsmanship.

In this society the most important personage was the warrior king, whose wandering existence was a result of his chief duty, the leading of his people to war. This the pagan kings of the West Saxons did with much success and when they and their people were converted to Christianity the resulting alliance between Church and State helped to secure Wessex's supremacy over the other Anglo-Saxon kingdoms. The conversion of Hampshire to Christianity was begun in A.D. 634 by St. Birinus, whose mission is briefly referred to in Bede, in the *Anglo-Saxon Chronicle* and in a number of 'lives' of the Saint composed hundreds of years after his task was accomplished. Bede, an Englishman, whose chief complaint about the conquered Britons was their refusal to try to convert the pagan Saxons, described Birinus as converting the Gewissae (or West Saxons), who were completely heathen, and this may well mean that Christianity had disappeared from Hampshire after the withdrawal of the Romans. Birinus too, according to one authority, was a Roman priest who was commissioned by Pope Honorius I to preach Christianity in those parts of England which had not received the Gospel. He may have landed at Portchester, was certainly kindly received by the King of the West Saxons, Cynegils, and in A.D. 635 baptized him, a very important event indeed but one not followed by the conversion of all the royal family. Cynegil's second son, his successor, Cenwealh, was not yet a baptized Christian when he began to build the great church called the Old Minster in Winchester in 642. Three years later he was temporarily driven out of his kingdom by Penda of Mercia and was baptized only in 646 when in exile at the court of his Christian host, King Anna of the East Angles. According to the *Chronicle*, the conversion of the Isle of Wight

1. Portchester Castle; the keep, *c.* 1160, and the walls, part of which date from the Roman fortress of *Portus Adurni*; centre background the church of the Augustinian Canons (*c.* 1133), now the parish church.

2. Roman Altar found in Jewry Street, Winchester in 1854.

3. Bronze figurine of the guardian spirit of the family from a shrine at *Calleva Atrebatum.*

4. St. Swithun of Winchester (d. 862) from the Benedictional of St. Ethelwold.

5. King Edgar offers his charter for New-minster, 966.

6. Seal of Aelfric, Ealdorman of Hampshire (killed 1016): found at Weeke, Winchester.

7. Leather binding of the Winchester Surveys of 1110 and 1148.

followed that of the mainland but it was the work of a missionary priest, Eoppa, undertaken at the request of the exiled Bishop Wilfrid of Northumbria. In the same year, the Island was 'harried' by Penda's Christian son, Wulfhere, who gave it to his godson, the king of the South Saxons.

In the early years of the Christian Church in Hampshire Birinus as bishop ruled a diocese which had its centre at Dorchester-on-Thames. The growing importance of Winchester and particularly the presence of a large, royally endowed church, resulted eventually in the moving of the bishop's Chair (*Cathedra*) there in about A.D. 676, by Bishop Haedda, who also brought Birinus's body to Winchester, the first of many relics of English saints revered in the Old Minster. The close connection of the bishops with the royal family of Wessex undoubtedly made easier the work of conversion in Hampshire, yet it was a long time before every Hampshire village had its own church. The Gospel was probably preached from free-standing preaching crosses, of which fragments of only a few remain, and the Christian community was served by groups of priests working from fairly large churches known as 'Mynsters'. There was a Minster at Wic (near Southampton), a Minster at Twynham (Christchurch), a Minster at Wimborne on the edge of the New Forest, and a minster for nuns as well as the Cathedral Minster in Winchester, where Edward the Elder carried out the wish of his father, Alfred, by adding yet a third royal foundation, the New Minster, St. Grimbald's Abbey, consecrated in 903. Though it was a great part of Alfred's life work to re-establish Christian learning after the ravages of the Danes, a further revival and re-establishment was necessary by the middle of the tenth century. Bishop Ethelwold (963–984) a monk himself, replaced the secular priests of the Old and New Minsters by monks of the reformed Cluniac Benedictine order, and virtually refounded and re-endowed the two Hampshire Benedictine nunneries of Romsey and St. Mary's, Winchester. Many of the early bishops were monks, but parish priests were not always celibate. Generous royal gifts of relics, money and landed endowments either directly to the various monastic houses, or the diocesan bishops, soon helped to turn the Anglo-Saxon Church in Hampshire into one of the wealthiest and largest dioceses in England; at first, the diocese was very large indeed, but by the reign of Edward the Elder, the creation of other sees reduced the area subject to the Bishops of Winchester and the diocese consisted, more or less, of the present counties of Surrey and Hampshire.

Further reading : Saxon Architecture in Hampshire, A. R. and P. M. Green (Warren & Son, 1951).
(Gives a very clear picture of parish churches of this period.)
The Anglo-Saxon Chronicle, ed. D. Whitelock, D. Douglas, and S. Tucker (Eyre & Spottiswoode, 1901).
'Winchester Cathedral in the tenth century', R. N. Quirk (*Royal Archaeological Institute Journal.* CXIV).
An Introduction to Anglo-Saxon England, by P. H. Blair (C.U.P., 1960).
Anglo-Saxon England, F. M. Stenton (Clarendon Press, 2nd Edition, 1946).
The Archaeology of Wessex, Chapter XV, 'The Saxon Invasion', L. V. Grinsell (Methuen, 1958).

IV

Anglo-Saxon Hampshire

THE conversion of Anglo-Saxon England to Christianity was not followed by a period of peace or by political unity. For many years the country was harassed by internal wars and political power varied with the personality and military success of the local kings. In the eighth century the great central kingdom of Mercia became very strong, but after the death of Offa of Mercia in A.D. 796 Wessex became the leading kingdom, and its kings united England and drove back the new invaders, men from Scandinavia, usually called Danes or Vikings. Wessex had powerful neighbours, but King Egbert who died in A.D. 839 succeeded in annexing Kent, was overlord of Mercia, harried Cornwall and was recognized as Bretwalda, 'ruler of the British'. When southern England was again troubled by invaders in the middle of the ninth century, it was Egbert's son Ethelwulf and the most famous of his grandsons, Alfred, who organized the opposition and eventually drove back the Danes. After Alfred made peace with the Danes in A.D. 877 and their leader Guthrum was baptized, many Danes remained in England in the area known as the Danelaw, but Alfred's military successes made possible the blossoming of Anglo-Saxon civilization, and established the political importance of Wessex.

The kingdom of Wessex consisted of a number of shires, and the historic existence of Hampshire goes back to at least A.D. 757. In that year, according to the *Anglo-Saxon Chronicle*, King Sigberht, who had ruled badly, was deprived of most of his kingdom except for 'Hamtunscire'. The shire presumably derives its name from Hamtun, the Anglo-Saxon settlement in the south of the county and the predecessor of the medieval town of Southampton. Significantly it was not called after the centre of the diocese,

Winchester (*Wintanceaster*) though that cathedral city later became the county town. By the time of Alfred, local government in Hampshire, as in other Wessex shires, was the responsibility of an official known as an ealdorman who also had to lead the men of his shire in time of war as did the ealdorman Wulfheard who routed the Danish attack on Southampton in A.D. 840. Ealdormen were royal officials, sometimes members of the royal family, but they often had their own local estates, and their local knowledge was of help when they administered the King's laws and presided over the shire's court. At least one ealdorman of Wessex, Aelfric, had his own personal seal; it was he who betrayed the army to the Danes in 992 and again in 1003 and who was killed at Ashingdon in 1016.

Much of what is known of Anglo-Saxon society is derived from the various codes of laws compiled by successive kings of Wessex and political history is contained in the *Anglo-Saxon Chronicle*, a great chronological record written down in the vernacular, of which the earliest surviving manuscript has a particular Hampshire interest, for much of it was written in Winchester, probably in the Old Minster. The use of the Anglo-Saxon language for codes of law and for the writing of history did much to encourage the feeling that England under the leadership of the royal house of Wessex was becoming a nation, and the feeling of national pride was encouraged by Alfred's successes against the Danes, by the growth of English towns, and by a revival and reorganization within the national Church.

In Hampshire it is clear that there were important towns at Southampton and at Winchester. The centre which gave the shire its name, Hamtun, was not on the site of the later medieval and present town, but appears to have been composed of two districts on the peninsula of land lying between the Rivers Test and Itchen. It has been suggested that the prefix 'South' was added to distinguish two parts of the settled area from each other, and not to distinguish the town from Northampton in another county. On the Test side perhaps stood Hamtun, but its site has not been identified. On the shores of a lagoon formed by the Itchen stood Hamwic, the commercial area of the town, perhaps as its name may suggest, a trading suburb of the fortified main settlement. Hamwic had a Minster church, the 'Minster at Wic' being the original of the church later dedicated to St. Mary, the mother church of modern Southampton. Hamwic, described as a *Mercimonium*, was convenient for trade with the Continent, and recent archaeological excavations have resulted in the discovery of jars and flagons for wine-carrying, and fine imported glass ware. Yet its position was very vulnerable; Ealdorman Wulfheard was able to defeat a Viking attack on Hamwic in 840, but in 980 a very severe raid resulted in the slaughter or captivity of most of the population.

The Viking raids on Southampton, and the fact that the bishop's Chair was at Winchester were both factors which helped to increase the importance of the cathedral city. Yet very little indeed is known of Winchester as an Anglo-Saxon centre before the reign of Edward the Confessor. Like Southampton, it was a *burh*, or fortified centre to be defended against the Danes, a place of resistance and refuge in time of trouble. The system is described in a document called the Burghal Hidage, dating from the reign of Edward the Elder—though the idea probably originated with his father Alfred, and listing the centres which were to be fortified and the number of men required to man them. In Hampshire there were *burhs* at Winchester, Southampton, Twynham and in the Roman port of Portchester, the last a late addition to the system. A recent interpretation of the Winchester evidence suggests that

the fortification of the *burh* coincides with the line of the Roman-medieval wall and needed some 2,400 men to man its total length of nearly two miles. All that can be added with any degree of certainty of Winchester in the hundred years after Alfred's death is that the layout of the town was dominated by two factors. The group of three royally founded minster churches already referred to occupied much of the area on the south side of the High Street, and secondly, the presence of the river Itchen and of many brooks was an important factor in the topography of the city. It is also reasonable to assume that the Anglo-Saxon kings had some sort of residence in Winchester and that their hall or palace was not far from the three minsters. There were undoubtedly other royal residences within the county, for example perhaps at Andover where Edgar made part of his Law, and where Ethelred the Unready stood as sponsor to Olaf of Norway in 994 in a period of temporary peace with the Danish invaders, and perhaps also at Twynham, where there was a 'residence'.

Later on, for a short period in the first half of the eleventh century England was ruled by Danish kings, a period of considerable growth and prosperity in Hampshire. Cnut, his wife Emma (widow of Ethelred the Unready) and their son Hardicanute were all buried in the Old Minster at Winchester, one of the many Anglo-Saxon foundations enriched by the Danish royal family in England. In 1043 the old line of English kings was restored by the coronation in Winchester Cathedral of Edward the Confessor, the son of Emma by her first marriage.

It was a measure of the vitality and integrity of Anglo-Saxon civilization that it was able to withstand and even in some ways to profit from the prolonged struggles with the Danes. To this civilization Hampshire made an important and considerable contribution. The two royal monasteries at Winchester became the fountain heads of a moving and magnificent style of manuscript illumination and writing which is now known

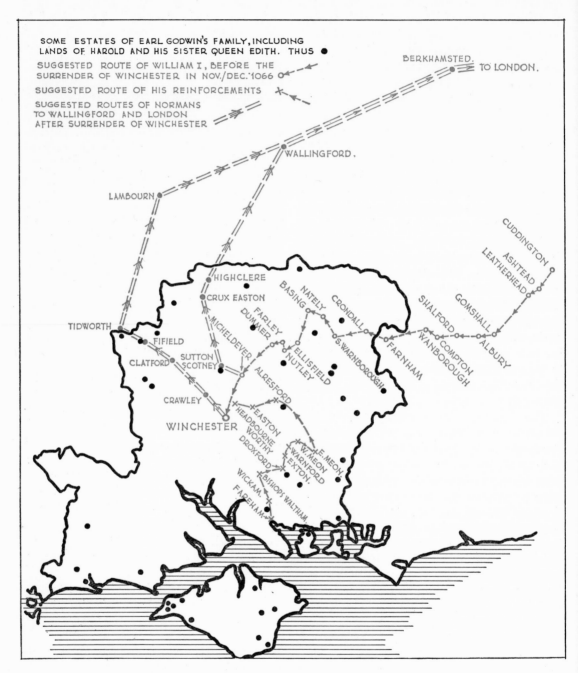

SOME ESTATES OF EARL GODWIN'S FAMILY, INCLUDING
LANDS OF HAROLD AND HIS SISTER QUEEN EDITH. THUS ●

SUGGESTED ROUTE OF WILLIAM I, BEFORE THE
SURRENDER OF WINCHESTER IN NOV./DEC. '1066 ○

SUGGESTED ROUTE OF HIS REINFORCEMENTS

SUGGESTED ROUTES OF NORMANS
TO WALLINGFORD AND LONDON
AFTER SURRENDER OF WINCHESTER

BERKHAMSTED.

TO LONDON.

WALLINGFORD.

LAMBOURN

CUDDINGTON

ASHTEAD

LEATHERHEAD

HIGHCLERE

CRUX EASTON

NATELY

BASING

CRONDALL

SHALFORD

GOMSHALL

FARLEY

DUMMER

S. WARNBOROUGH

MICHELDEVER

ELLISFIELD

NUTLEY

FARNHAM

COMPTON

WANBOROUGH

ALBURY

TIDWORTH

FIFIELD

CLATFORD

SUTTON

SCOTNEY

ALRESFORD

CRAWLEY

EASTON

WINCHESTER

HEADBOURNE

WORTHY

E. MEON

DROXFORD

W. MEON

WARNFORD

EXTON.

WICKAM.

BISHOPS WALTHAM

FAREHAM.

Map 3.   Hampshire estates of the Godwin family c. 1065 and possible route of the Norman Army.

all over the civilized world as the 'Winchester School'. Its most famous example is the Benedictional of St. Ethelwold, commissioned by that bishop and known to have been at Hyde Abbey (Newminster) in the later medieval period, though it may have been made in the Old Minster or indeed in one of the monasteries outside Hampshire reformed by Bishop Ethelwold's influence. The great minster churches themselves were renowned examples of contemporary architecture, richly decorated and famous for their music. Indeed, their outstanding contribution to England's musical history, the Winchester 'tropes', ornamental additions to plainsong music which went out of fashion after 1066, can be recalled today from the existence of two rare manuscripts, the Winchester trophers. A less formal kind of music was envisaged in the special provision which the church made for the particularly English custom of pealing bells, provision confirmed at the great national synod held in Winchester in *c.* 970, a synod which apparently met at Bishop Ethelwold's request and issued the *Regularis Concordia*, an agreed rule for general use in all English monastries.

The language of the Church was Latin, which was also often used for some formal documents and charters concerning land. Yet the language of the ordinary people was alive and already so strong in use that it was able to survive the Norman Conquest, to conquer French, and emerge at the end of the Middle Ages as the language of English society. Its strength was helped by the translations of King Alfred, by the continued existence of the *Chronicle*, by the fact that Anglo-Saxon was used in many charters and official documents and that it was also the language of some serious scholarship. Wulfstan of Winchester wrote descriptive poems about his monastery and its music; Alfric the Grammarian (*c.* 980—*c.* 1020) compiled vast quantities of original homilies for feast days, lives of saints, and sermons for all occasions.

The civilization of Anglo-Saxon Christian Hampshire was thus vigorous and manifold and was never insular nor merely local. Trade with Western Europe flourished, and with Scandinavia, the Anglo-Saxon Church, though it had its peculiarities, was part of Christendom. It was a monk from Nursling, near Southampton, St. Boniface, who, in a series of great missionary journeys, preached Christianity to the Frisians before his martyrdom at their hands in 754. Boniface had the help and encouragement of the Bishop of Winchester, Daniel, and of the Pope; regular contacts were always maintained with the Papal Curia. There were frequent contacts too, with France; the first Abbot of Newminster, St. Grimbald, was a Frenchman. Emma, mother of Edward the Confessor, sister of Duke Richard of Normandy and 'the Gem of the Normans', spent much of her widowhood at Wherwell and in Winchester after the death of her second husband, Cnut. When her son Edward the Confessor was crowned King of England in Winchester Cathedral in 1043, Winchester was no longer merely the chief town in Wessex but had become the royal capital of Anglo-Saxon England.

Further reading: *The Anglo-Saxon Chronicle*, ed. D. Whitelock, D. Douglas and S. Tucker (Eyre & Spottiswoode, 1961).

Late Saxon and Viking Art, T. D. Kendrick, (Methuen, 1949).

'Southampton before the Norman Conquest', M. R. Maitland Muller, in *Southampton Essays*, (Southampton Corporation, 1958).

The Benedictional of St. Ethelwold, F. Wormald (Faber & Faber, 1960).

Liber Vitae: New Minster and Hyde Abbey, ed. W. De G. Birch (Hampshire Record Society, 1892).

'Trinity Chapel and Fair', O. G. S. Crawford (H.F.C. *Proceedings*, XVII, pt. 1. 1949). (Important for its consideration of the site of Saxon Southampton.)

'The Topogrophy of Alfred's Wars in Wessex', J. P. Williams Freeman (H.F.C. *Proceedings*, XVIII, Pt. 1953).

V

The Hampshire Domesday (1)

The county in the reign of Edward the Confessor
(1043–66)

IN the eleventh century the office of ealdorman of the county declined in importance.
Instead, the most important layman in
Hampshire was the Earl (*comes*) of Wessex, a
nobleman with great estates who left the
routine work of administration to his deputy
(*vice-comes*) the shire reeve (sheriff) of Hampshire. In the reign of Edward the Confessor
(1043–66) the most powerful man of Wessex
was Earl Godwin, whose daughter Edith
married the King, and whose second son,
Harold, was the famous last Anglo-Saxon
king of England. Twenty years after Harold's
defeat and death at Hastings, William the
Conqueror caused to be compiled his great
Domesday Survey. 'Domesday Book' consists of two volumes of which the smaller,
'Little Domesday', is concerned only with
East Anglia; the larger survey covers all the
other counties, including Hampshire. This
survey is of paramount importance in the
history of the county for its object was to
furnish detailed information of the financial
and economic condition of Hampshire not
only as it was in 1086, but as it had been at
the end of the reign of the Confessor, 'on the
day when King Edward was alive and dead',
and also to note the value of landed estates if
and when they had been re-granted by King
William earlier in his reign. The plan of
the Inquiry is very simple. Hampshire was
surveyed under the names of the great owners
of land, including the King himself; within
each personal estate thus described the
county was further divided into Hundreds.
Each Hundred had its own ancient name and
its own local court, and within each Hundred
the basic holding was the manor, which
varied in size and in the geld which it paid.
Though this division is not without difficulty

and meant, for example, that in order to construct a picture of any particular Hundred,
the whole survey had to be used, the record as
a whole is complete and efficient, the greatest
single achievement of all early English administration. When it was finished it was kept
in the Treasury at Winchester, by royal
command. The King's instructions to his
Commissioners have survived, and it is clear
from their orders and from the results of their
work that they were required to obtain as detailed an account of each manor as was possible, who the inhabitants were, if they paid
geld direct to the King or if it was paid by the
lord of the manor, how much land there was,
whether it was wooded or meadow, or pasture, if there was a mill and if there was a
church. This survey of manors and their
holders thus provides the social and economic basis of the essential political feudalism
by which the Conqueror ruled his kingdom.
All the information was supplied by juries
from each Hundred, and other men too,
the sheriff of the county, reeves, priests, who
gave additional evidence on oath if required
to do so.

In the Hampshire of Edward the Confessor, the King himself was the most important
landed proprietor, and his most important
separate estate was the city of Winchester,
where his position in some respects was
that of general landlord to the burgesses
of the city. Their distinctive burgess tenure
was essentially their free right to let and to sell
their freehold property provided they gave
due notice in the borough court. Property
held by burgess tenure in this way paid the
King a 'gablum', a rent for each house-
gable, and the duty of paying gablum passed
with the property from owner to owner. It

was still being assessed in Winchester in the eighteenth century, as tarrage. Edward the Confessor obtained this rent from sixty-three burgesses, but this information is not in Domesday Book. Winchester, the capital of England, was probably too large a town to fit into the general survey and, like London, was left out. Special surveys of the town made in 1110 and 1148, bound together in one volume, the so-called Winchester Domesday, make good this earlier deficiency. On the eve of the Norman Conquest Winchester was a flourishing city. On the north side of the High Street stood two halls of 'Chenictes', gilds of knights whose function was perhaps to defend the city. The eastern hall can be identified as the later St. John's House; the other, western, hall was on a site which was fronted by shops belonging to Newminster, approached by a lane off the High Street, at the rear of the building which is now No. 85 High Street. Near the Westgate was a house which belonged to the King's consort, Godwin's daughter, farther down the High Street were the minters and moneyers, makers of the king's coin, the money of England, Aelfwine, Aitwardesonne, Alestan and Andrebod, as well as Godwin Socche, the master moneyer. Local government in Winchester was still very much controlled by the frequent presence of the king, but its beginning is indicated by the mention of Winchester reeves and street beadles. This information and much else about Anglo-Saxon Winchester is to be found in the earlier of the two Winchester surveys, which compares the town as it was in 1110 with what it had been in the time of King Edward. To it may be added some occasional references which occur in Domesday Book proper, when the city is mentioned because certain county landowners have financial interests in it, for example the Abbess of Wherwell who had a mill and thirty-one messuages, and the Abbess of Romsey who also had burgesses in Winchester.

Though the other boroughs of Twynham and Southampton are both individually de-scribed in the Survey of 1086, the account given of them is very scanty. Perhaps Hamton was still on its early Anglo-Saxon site, and not fully recovered from its sacking of 980. Yet its burgesses, apparently seventy-six in number, paid £7 gablum to the King. The rebuilding of the town may have been begun in Cnut's time, in an area now represented by the medieval walled town. The mother church remained the minster at South Stoneham.

In the country generally King Edward's royal demesne, the manors which he had not let to a tenant, varied in size and in value and were scattered over Hampshire and the Isle of Wight. He had land at Basingstoke, Hurstbourne, Andover, Wymering, Portchester, Rockbourne, King's Somborne, Titchfield and Twyford. His queen drew revenues from Anstey near Alton, Greatham, Selborne, Upton, Kingsclere and Penton Grafton. Her father, the Earl of Wessex, and her brothers were all richly endowed with Hampshire revenues, but the Godwin fortunes varied with politics. The earl was banished for a short time in 1051 and though he was back at the King's table in 1053 his death in that year and at that table was considered by many to be a fit punishment for his alleged part in the murder of the King's brother, Alfred. The Winchester annalist compiling the chronicle which was kept in the Old Minster recorded the event with brevity, "'May this crumb choke me,' said Earl Godwin, 'If I killed your brother' ... and he died." Godwin's second son, Harold, succeeded him as Earl of Wessex.

Amongst other prominent lay landowners were royal 'thegns' and courtiers. One of them, Odo de Winchestre, had property which included land in the Isle of Wight and at Chawton, and his brother Eldred was tenant at Micheldever of Newminster and of the Bishop of Winchester. Perhaps the most important of the thegns was Cheping of Worthy who had thirteen manors as well as two houses in Winchester and three in Southampton.

The estates of lay owners might vary with political change. Manors owned by ecclesiastics were not usually subject to such political hazards and in Hampshire a fundamental and unchanging feature of the economy of the county even as recently as the mid-nineteenth century was the large proportion of land, the many manors, owned by the Church. Chief amongst these ecclesiastical owners was the Bishop of Winchester himself. It was the wealth of the Anglo-Saxon bishopric which made it possible for Bishop Ethelwold to rebuild the Cathedral Church of the old monastery in Winchester, and for later, medieval, bishops to make it a storehouse of countless treasures. It is not yet really clear at what historical point there occurred a main division of the bishop's property into those manors which provided the resources and revenue of the bishoprics and those which were for the 'support of the monks', that is, for the cathedral and priory church of St. Swithun in Winchester. The bishop's own manors and those of the priory made up the two major landed estates in the county, much of the land being of royal gift of considerable antiquity; of manor after manor it is recorded in Domesday that it belonged to the bishop or that it was always the minster's. Very few private donations are recorded, one interesting exception being the gift (to Newminster) of land at Tatchbury in Eling by the sheriff, Ezi, a gift made for King Edward's soul.

Other Hampshire monasteries had smaller but also valuable estates, Newminster, the canons of Twynham, the nuns of St. Mary's (Winchester), Romsey and Wherwell. Many of these ecclesiastical manors were kept in demesne, that is worked directly by the monastery concerned, through its own local lay officials; the minority were let to lay tenants at money rents, though rents in kind were not unknown. Newminster let Comer in Corhampton for an annual rent of wine, perhaps from grapes grown locally, especially since wine is produced today in nearby Hambledon. It is this aspect of Domesday, the use which it records of the land, which makes it so important as a source of Hampshire's social and economic history. Though the main unit was the manor, that term was applied in many different ways. The huge Priory manor of Chilcomb stretched for many miles round Winchester. Other manors were obviously smaller districts; some are said to have had halls, perhaps the predecessors of what were later and often wrongly called 'manor houses'. Thus there were two halls at Warnford, two at Clere, three at Knapp, in Christchurch, one at Portchester, with its own fishery, one at Boarhunt with its own mill.

With the many mills and churches they formed the only permanent buildings in or near the poor and squalid hovels which made up the majority of buildings in Hampshire Anglo-Saxon villages. It is clear that there was much mixed farming and that rivers and forest played an important part in the county's economy. Forests were not merely waste places where the nobility could hunt; forest land fed swine and produced honey, timber and rough pasture for cattle. Hampshire's many rivers were also a valuable asset to those whose estates contained them. Hay, from water meadows, and fish, including eels, were only part of this riverside wealth and the production of flour, from differing kinds of grains, depended almost entirely on the existence of many rivers with water-mills.

Further reading: The Domesday Geography of South-East England, ed. by H. C. Darby and E. M. J. Campbell (C.U.P., 1962).
Hampshire, Chapter VII, by E. Welldon Finn.

The Hampshire Domesday (2)

The effect of the Norman Conquest

SOME few weeks after the battle of Hastings, Winchester surrendered to William the Conqueror, a submission apparently sent by Queen Edith, the Confessor's widow, who was living in the city. It is not absolutely certain when William I first came into Hampshire, but one of his first acts in Winchester was to demolish the houses of twelve burgesses and to build himself a palace in the centre of the High Street, on this site and on other land taken from New-minster. A Domesday jury noted that this latter part of the site was already royal property and that William had therefore no need to compensate the Abbey with other land at Kingsclere and at Alton. In any case, the life of this palace was short, for it appears to have been destroyed in the civil war of Stephen's reign, when the triumphant diocesan bishop, Henry de Blois, used the materials to rebuild his own palace-castle at Wolvesey. The site in the High Street was difficult to defend and by the reign of Henry II there was a royal fortress on the western hill, Winchester Castle, where the last Anglo-Saxon bishop of Winchester, Stigand, died as a prisoner in 1070. Of this castle the most impressive reminder today is the great hall, now in use as an Assize Court. Even more majestic is the cathedral, a massive demonstration of the impact of the Conquest, for the first Norman bishop of the diocese, Walkelin, completely demolished the Anglo-Saxon church and his new building retains its Norman framework beneath later additions and alterations. The architectural and engineering skill of the Normans enabled them to construct a huge church on a very poor foundation, but the central tower soon collapsed and was replaced after 1100 by a second structure of much finer and more substantial masonry in the later Romanesque style. Simple round-headed arches, rounded columns, and lack of ornament and small slit windows are the significant features which distinguish the smaller Hampshire churches rebuilt in the Norman and Romanesque periods. Much of this building was done in Caen stone quarried in Normandy and imported to Hampshire via Southampton.

The power of the Normans and the military nature of the Conquest soon made itself felt all over the county. At Southampton a new royal castle was erected on a mound overlooking the western shore, for the town was an important embarkation point for kings whose dominions were on both sides of the English Channel. Southampton Castle was not only a strong point but it was also a royal storehouse, great quantities of wine being imported and kept in huge vaults within the castle precincts. Outside of these precincts the town grew rapidly on its new site and according to Domesday Book, the population had very greatly increased by the Norman Conquest. To a total of some seventy to eighty burgesses of Anglo-Saxon origin was added sixty-five French- and thirty-one English-speaking families, whose coming greatly increased the town's prosperity and whose presence also resulted in a linguistic division, for the main streets soon became known as French and English Streets. Many merchants in both Winchester and Southampton were probably bi-lingual, for a striking feature of town life in Hampshire at this time was the easy and frequent communication with French-speaking merchants from the other side of the Channel. By the first half of the twelfth century there was a resident Jewish community in Winchester. As this community developed and grew in size its members maintained a close connection with Normandy, and the majority of Hampshire Jews in Southampton, in Romsey and in Portsmouth probably continued to speak French. Norman-French was the language of the great Norman Plantaganet Civil Service, though Latin, the language of the Church, was much used for administrative records. The Hampshire peasant and the poorer townspeople continued to speak English, but there must have been many bi-lingual families.

The changes brought about by the Conquest were not confined to architecture and language. The most important effects on the county as a whole include the growth of town life in all its aspects, the development of a strong central government administration and the handing over of estates to new Norman landowners. The development of Hampshire towns is considered in a later chapter, but here it may be noted that the conquest had an immediate effect on Hampshire landlords. The power of Earl Godwin's family was broken, though his daughter, the Old Lady, Queen Edith, continued to live on in Winchester until her death in 1070. William I succeeded to the ancient demesne land of Edward the Confessor, and to these the Crown added other property by forfeiture or by death; the land of the 'Old Lady', estates from Bishop Stigand, and the Hampshire lands of the rebellious Earl Roger of Hereford. Only a few Hampshire thegns withstood the storm of the Conquest, amongst them Odo of Winchester, who lost land in the Isle of Wight and in Chawton, but who had acquired by 1086 five Hampshire houses which had previously belonged to other Englishmen in the reign of King Edward. Cheping of Worthy was not so fortunate, for the greater part of his estate was given to Ralf de Mortimer, though he may have been allowed a very small holding at Candover. By the time Domesday Book was written the greatest of the new Hampshire lay landlords was Hugh de Port, who was apparently a vassal of Bishop Odo of Bayeux;

throughout the county he held about fifty-six manors direct from the Crown, thirteen as a tenant of the Bishop of Bayeux, a great 'fief' which had a long existence remaining intact for many years in the hands of his heirs, the de Ports and the St. Johns. This fief had its centre or *caput* at Basing, where the manor house was later rebuilt by the first Marquess of Winchester and in the time of the fifth Marquess gained fame as 'Loyalty House', the centre of Royalist resistance during the Civil War. One of the secondary residences of the de Port family was at Warnford and the ruined remnant of this building is a rare example in Hampshire of a great early medieval stone hall-house.

The Conqueror's grant to Newminster of land at Kingsclere and Alton has already been mentioned. He also gave that abbey an estate at Laverstoke for the sake of his soul and that of his queen, Matilda, and there is indeed no evidence, as has been suggested, that William disliked Newminster or tried to impoverish it. Not one of the old Anglo-Saxon monastic foundations suffered permanent loss of endowment as a result of the Conquest, and, moreover, certain important Norman monasteries were also endowed with Hampshire estates, Jumieges receiving land at Hayling Island, and Mont St. Michael the very rich living of Basingstoke. The bishopric of Winchester and the monks of the Cathedral Church continued to be exceptionally rich and part of their incomes was used for the rebuilding of Winchester Cathedral and the construction of new and larger parish churches.

The Conqueror and his sons were frequently in Hampshire. William I continued the ancient custom, at least as old as Cnut's reign, of 'wearing his Crown' in Winchester at Eastertide; two of his sons were killed in the New Forest and both were buried in Winchester Cathedral. One of these sons was William Rufus and after his death it was to Winchester that his brother and successor, Henry I, came, to make sure of the royal treasure, and it was from a Hampshire nunnery, Romsey, that he took his English wife, Edith, and thus united the line of the Anglo-Saxon and Norman royal families. After Henry I's death it was the military struggle for Winchester which became a vital point in the civil war between his daughter Matilda and her rival, Stephen de Blois, whose chief supporter was his brother Henry, Bishop of Winchester. Fierce and brutal though the civil war was, this period of anarchy at length paved the way for the return of strong government under Henry II.

The strength and success of Norman and Plantagenet administration depended essentially on the efficiency of the King's local representatives. Domesday Book mentions an Anglo-Saxon Sheriff of Hampshire, Ezi, but it was the Normans' great contribution to efficient local government that they made great use of the system by which each county was ruled by its sheriff. Strictly speaking the sheriff, 'vice-comes'

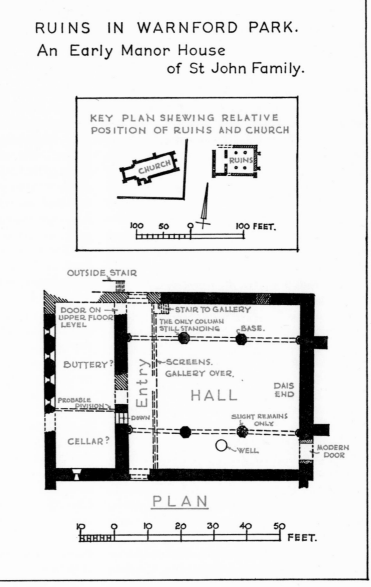

Map 4. *A Manor House of the de Port, later St. John, family in Warnford Park.*

of the county, was the deputy of the 'comes', the earl of the county, though in fact there were never earls of Hampshire and the earldom of Wessex died with Harold at Hastings. The sheriff of Hampshire, responsible to the King for county finance and for the maintenance of law and order, also presided over the county court, visited the courts of the various Hampshire Hundreds and held views of 'frankpledge' in the tithings into which the Hundreds were divided. He received the royal commands in the form of writs and precepts directing that certain actions be taken, and it was his duty to see that these writs were carried out, as well as to make the arrangements for holding Assizes, special sittings of the King's justices held in certain towns. The Hampshire Assize town was and is Winchester where the Courts are presided over by judges, though in the early medieval period the sheriff himself was often the most active member amongst many named on the Assize Commission, which usually included a number of local magnates and important ecclesiastics. It was the sheriff's duty to collect the King's revenue due from Hampshire, including the farms or towns (made up chiefly of burgesses' gable rents) and also to pay out from the money received any necessary local expenditure incurred on behalf of the King or other members of the royal family. These sheriff's accounts, of receipts and expenditure, had to be audited twice a year, at Easter and at Michaelmas on behalf of the department of the royal civil service which soon became known as the Exchequer and the accounts for each year were written up in Latin in a great formal record known as the Pipe Roll. The Pipe Rolls continue as a series from the reign of Henry II but the existence of a roll for 1130 shows that the system goes back to an earlier period. The Pipe Rolls are thus a primary source for the history of Hampshire. The records are well named, as they show the way in which money flowed from each county into the royal purse. The money itself was kept in the Treasury, which remained at Winchester till about the end of the twelfth century, when it was moved to Westminster, but very large sums were still left in Hampshire in the reigns of John and Henry III, and it has been pointed out that on one occasion in 1208 nearly six and a half million pennies had to be counted in the Winchester Treasury.

The section on the Pipe Rolls dealing with Hampshire is headed with the name of the county and usually has certain well-defined sub-divisions, *Hamptona* (Southampton), *Civitatis Wintonie* (Winchester) as well as being a kind of general balance sheet of expenditure and receipts. Thus the sheriff in 1167–68, Richard Fitz Turstin, paid the royal alms to the Knights Templar, gave the Queen an allowance, received payments from debtors and tenants including the Bishop of Winchester, the Abbot of Hyde and the Abbess of Romsey and accounted for various payments made to provide ships for the royal family's Channel crossings. In 1176 the Pipe Rolls show the sheriff accounting for a large number of fines levied on Hampshire men who had infringed forest law. Hampshire sheriffs were usually county gentlemen, with property in the shire but of the professional civil service class rather than great magnates. A late thirteenth-century example is Sir Simon de Winton, sheriff in 1283, who had been Mayor of Winchester in 1266 and other years and who had property in the city as well as being lord of the Hampshire manors of Otterbourne and Lainston. Though the office was often profitable and there were plenty of opportunities to extort money unjustly and to benefit from bribery and corruption, nevertheless, under a strong king, local county government, administered by the sheriff was reasonably efficient and justice was done.

Further reading: The Domesday Geography of South-East England, edited by H. C. Darby and E. M. J. Campbell (C.U.P., 1962).
'William the Conqueror's March through Hampshire in 1066', F. B. Baring (H.F.C. *Proceedings*, Vol: VII. Pt: II, 1915).
Pipe Roll, 1167–1168 (Pipe Roll Society, 1890) and subsequent volumes.

VII

The Towns of Medieval Hampshire

THOUGH the towns of medieval Hampshire had certain problems in common, problems of constitutional growth and of the development of local government, each flourishing community was also very different from the other, illustrating in many ways the differing social and economic aspects of civic life. The sheriff of the county was not normally popular in Hampshire towns and there was a general wish to exclude him, though his power was strong and his duties of preserving law and order and collecting royal revenue through town bailiffs gave him frequent opportunities for interfering in municipal affairs. With the King's consent the sheriff could be excluded from towns which obtained permission to collect the royal revenues and make their own financial returns to the Exchequer as a fixed rent or 'farm'. This right, to return the farm, was granted by royal charter; when it was a grant in perpetuity, known as a 'fee-farm', a very important stage in local constitutional development had been reached.

The movement towards independence was encouraged by the diminution of royal authority in the troubles of Stephen's reign (1135–54), by the need to encourage urban revival in the particular cases of Winchester and Andover, both of which were burnt and pillaged in the civil war, and by the example of certain French towns where the towns-people formed themselves into 'communes', headed by an officer known as the mayor. In some Hampshire towns this commune or commonalty led the movement towards independence. In other towns it was the Merchant Gild (a group of influential and wealthy townsmen which regulated trade and also met regularly for social and commercial reasons) which formed a nucleus of opposition to the sheriff and obtained charters of privileges from the King. These are such important points that it is worth-while examining them in the light of what actually happened in certain particular towns.

In Southampton the right of the gildsmen to form their own gild as they had done in the time of Henry I was confirmed by Henry II in 1154. Yet the charter of 1199 given by King John granted the fee-farm of the town, with that of Portsmouth, to the townsmen 'our men of Southampton', not to the gildsmen. The fee-farm was then fixed at the annual rent of £200. The first mention of a mayor of Southampton occurs before 1221, and a little later on, probably in 1236, a certain Benedict Ace became mayor: he apparently held office for a long period, but in October, 1249 the townspeople obtained a promise from Henry III that they should never again be governed by a mayor. For some years Southampton was again ruled by bailiffs, until 1267–8 when the Alderman of the gild was the chief officer. For the next fifty or sixty years the gild's was the chief voice in Southampton affairs, and the regular succession of mayors did not begin until 1333.

It was satisfactory for towns when they were able, by returning their own fee-farm, to exclude the sheriff of the county from their financial affairs, but he could still interfere to enforce the King's writs. Southampton reached a further stage of independence in 1447 when the town, by royal charter, became 'the county of the town of Southampton', with its own sheriff, as well as mayor, and therefore with the right to make returns of writs direct to the King himself or to his judicial officers. For this reason, Southampton enjoys a unique position in the later history of Hampshire towns: there is still a sheriff, who is always the mayor of the town in the year following his election as sheriff.

Inland from Southampton, the town of Andover had markedly similar constitutional characteristics, the earliest Andover charter being a grant to the Gild Merchant there by Henry II in 1175–6, confirmed by John in 1201 on payment of twenty marks and a palfrey. There are many later confirmations and, unlike Southampton, a very fine series of gild records which make a unique contribution to the county's medieval history, producing the most complete surviving account of a Merchant Gild from any Hampshire town. The Andover records show the gild to have been divided into two 'houses', an upper house, the 'free' gild, a lower house or villein or hanse gild. Regular meetings were held to appoint new members, make trade regulations and elect bailiffs. The bailiff's chief duty was to preside over an independent local court, dealing with the two districts into which Andover was divided, 'in hundred' and 'out hundred'. There was no mayor and no commune.

It is a significant fact that in these two towns, Andover and Southampton, where the power of the gild for so long a period was so important, the majority of the inhabitants depended directly upon commerce for their livelihoods. Southampton was a port, with a flourishing wine trade with France, and a varied coastal trade. Andover's importance in the medieval county was in the wool trade, for which the neighbouring Weyhill Fair was an important distribution centre. During the thirteenth century the wool trade was probably more important than the actual making of cloth, though cloth making was the subject of many regulations continually made by the gild.

Only three other Hampshire towns are known with certainty to have had Merchant Gilds besides those at Andover and Southampton, and in these, the towns of Petersfield, Portsmouth and Winchester, the pattern of constitutional development was different, the gild privileges and customs of Winchester being used as a model for the other two centres. Petersfield was a manorial

borough, belonging to William, Earl of Gloucester but its burgesses were free enough to gain in Henry II's reign the right of having a Merchant Gild on the model of that of Winchester. In Winchester the townspeople held their property as burgesses, with the right to dispose of their real estate as they wished without having to obtain permission from an overlord, and subject only to certain formalities in the city court. There was a Gild Merchant at least as early as the reign of Henry I, but the nucleus of free local government was also certainly to be found in the essential freedoms or burgess tenure, and in fact that a city court had to meet regularly. By 1155, there would appear to have been two groups in the city both able to negotiate charters from Henry II, who made one grant to his citizens of Winchester confirming their ancient privileges, and another to members of the Gild Merchant, including freedom from toll. A mayor of Winchester is referred to in 1200, but the Gild Merchant remained the most powerful group in civic affairs until about 1278. Though for a short period in 1155 the Winchester *prepositus* or reeve, Stigand, accounted for the city's farm direct to the Exchequer and not via the sheriff, it was perhaps difficult for a city whose townspeople were much dependent economically on the frequent presence of the King and his sheriff to sustain a continuous demand to manage its own financial affairs. Not until 1327 did Winchester obtain the right to return its fee-farm. Membership of the Winchester Gild remained the nominal way, but a formal way only, of becoming a freeman of the city until the reform of the Corporation in 1835. The earliest surviving copy of Winchester's local laws and trade regulations, the usages, was probably compiled in about 1278 after some months of disturbance and obvious dissension between the gild and non-gildsmen members of the Winchester Commune, and embodies many earlier customs and traditions. The gild had become a mere social club and in contrast to Andover, it was the Corporation of Winchester, the

Commonalty of Twenty-Four led by a mayor who regulated the all-important cloth industry. Many towns all over England regarded Winchester's particular and highly developed forms of local government as a model to be followed in their own endeavours to gain privileges by royal charter.

A complication and a hindrance to Portsmouth's growth was the claim of Southampton to include the town as being within the port of Southampton. Portsmouth's first charter was granted by Richard I in 1194, a grant illustrating that town's connection with Winchester, for the town was given a fair with the same liberties as those 'who attended the fairs at Winchester and Hoyland', and burgesses were to hold their tenants 'as freely as the citizens of Winchester and Oxford hold theirs'. In 1256 Portsmouth obtained the right to have a Gild Merchant, and the town's custumal or code of bye-laws, was finally drawn up at the end of the thirteenth century, a little later than its model, the Winchester Usages.

Amongst the smaller Hampshire towns, Basingstoke had no Merchant Gild but it was an important market centre for the north west of the county. The impressive ruins of the Chapel of the Gild of the Holy Ghost (once housing the members of an important

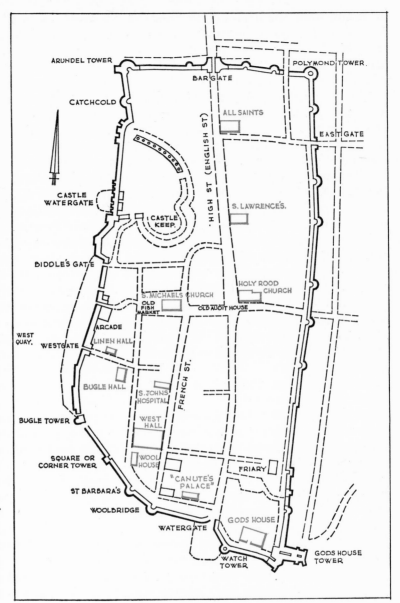

Map 5. Medieval Southampton.

religious gild, a community whose interests were not only commercial) are a reminder that religious gilds formed an important part of medieval life. Alresford was an episcopal, manorial, town which flourished very largely because of an annual fair granted by John to Bishop Godfrey de Lucy. Romsey was an important road centre, a little town which grew up in the shelter of a great abbey, its development obviously related to the grants of markets made to various Abbesses of Romsey by Henry I, Henry II and Henry III.

All Hampshire towns were closely united by their conscious knowledge of each other's constitutional development, embodied in royal charters granting privileges based on earlier similar grants to other towns, and by the economic ties of trade and commerce. Though many small towns and villages were virtually self-supporting, iron and salt were two vital commodities which had to be redistributed. Southampton was the great parent distributing centre of necessities and luxuries alike and the famous fair on St. Giles' Hill at Winchester provided a further opportunity for merchants to meet not only their Hampshire friends, but also traders from France, from Spain, the Low Countries and Italy, who sold wines, silks, strange fruits, pet monkeys and spices. The first sugar ever bought in England was purchased at Winchester in the reign of Henry III.

Every Hampshire town had, and still has, its own special features of topography and layout. Most of medieval Winchester was contained within a walled area pierced by five gates and at least one postern, a wall which probably followed the line of the Roman fortification. An early suburb outside the Westgate declined in importance as the area of the castle encroached on townspeople's houses. There were later suburban developments at Hyde, around the new buildings of Hyde Abbey, and to the south of the city in the area known as the Aldermanry of Kingsgate. Moreover, a vast part of the town outside of the eastern wall was under the jurisdiction of the Bishop of Winchester, and his 'Soke' was a place of refuge to those craftsmen, especially cloth workers, who wished to escape from the tiresome commercial regulations of the Corporation. The maintenance of the walls of Winchester was a fairly continual financial burden levied on the citizens by means of the wall tax or murage.

In Southampton the wall was of much later origin and the deficiencies of the defences was one of the reasons why the French were able to pillage and sack the town so completely in 1338. Yet poor as the defences were, in Southampton as well as in Winchester the medieval period, on the whole, was a period of commercial and industrial prosperity. There were many wealthy merchants who could build themselves houses of stone with a first-floor *solar*, amass large fortunes, and give away some of their money to the Church. In the twelfth century a Southampton merchant, Gervase de Hampton, lived in his great West Hall, a large house with an upper room with an oriel window, with a series of small buildings around it, surrounded by a high wall, and having its own pleasure garden. In Winchester, Thomas Palmer, alias Moraunt, a wealthy goldsmith had a rather more modest establishment in Calpe Street which was known as Moraunt's halle many years after Moraunt its builder had died. Marriage was often a business transaction leading to the accumulation of private fortunes and much real estate. The lady known as Dame Claramund who lived in a large house near St. Michael's Church at Southampton and who had two husbands, eventually owned a great many Southampton houses, and when she died in *c.* 1260 left part of her estate to God's House and to the Priory of St. Denys. The many Winchester properties of Hugh de Craan, Mayor of the city in 1357, 1365–6 and 1369–70 were partly the result of successful property speculations and partly the result of Craan's marriage with a county heiress, Isabella, the widow of John de Ingepenne.

The majority of townsfolk were not wealthy nor were they even very comfortably housed. Most town houses in Hampshire, not a 'stone' county, were of simple timber-framed construction with roofs of thatching of reeds or straw. In larger houses cooking was often done in a detached, single-storied kitchen in the back yard which was an inevitable feature of most town dwellings. Refuse was

8. The Cistercian Abbey at Netley showing (*left*) the church, (*centre*) the cloister garth and (*right*) the monastic kitchen.

9. The castle at Carisbrooke, Isle of Wight, showing the 16th-century gateway, and the 12th-century polygonal keep. Here Charles I was imprisoned from November 1647 till November 1648.

10. The Nave of Winchester Cathedral, looking west, showing William of Wykeham's alterations to the Norman fabric, and Edington's west window.

burnt, or buried in pits, or thrown out into the streets, though there were frequent attempts by the local authorities to prevent the more obvious abuses. Winchester forbade its burgesses to keep pigs in the High Street, its butchers to throw offal in the brooks, and all towns were supposed to enforce the national regulations concerning the quality of ale brewed and bread baked. All industrial processes, and all those people engaged in industry, whether as apprentices, journeymen, or master craftsmen, were subject in theory at least to stringent rules made by the local corporations or by the craft gilds, which eventually succeeded the Merchant Gild. Fines for industrial infringements were used to relieve needy brethren, help widows, or for social functions like the great torch-light procession of the craft gilds of Winchester on the Feast of Corpus Christi. Industry was domestic, carried on in the home, which was often a retail shop as well.

Before the Black Death, the majority of successful Hampshire merchants were probably general dealers, perhaps with large interests in the wholesale supply of wool or of wine, but ready to buy or sell anything in which they could see a useful profit. It was not always easy to know what to do with the large sums which they accumulated. After the expulsion of the Jews in 1290, and even before that date, some Hampshire Christians, the Dalrons for example, went into the moneylending business. Others bought pieces of silver plate and jewellery to pass down to their heirs; many more made bequests to the many religious houses and no man who made a will ever forgot his own parish church. For the majority of successful Hampshire townspeople it was simple and lucrative to invest in real property, either in the town or in the neighbouring countryside where many citizens bought or leased small country estates. Thus there was movement between town and country and since most Hampshire medieval towns by modern standards were but large villages there was much mutual understanding and sympathy between rustic and townsmen.

Further reading: *Catalogue of Historic Documents*, Portsmouth, 1956.

The Ancient Usages of the City of Winchester, J. S. Furley (Oxford, 1927).

Italian Merchants and Shipping in Southampton, 1270–1600, A. A. Ruddock (Southampton Record Society, 1951).

History of Southampton, J. S. Davies (Gilbert, 1883).

The Gild Merchant, Charles Gross.

Calendar of Charters of Winchester: ed. Herbert (Winchester, 1913).

Building in England Down to 1540, L. F. Salzman (Clarendon Press, 1952).
(Includes detailed building contracts for inns at Andover and Alresford, for repairs to Hartley Wintney Priory, and for new building in the city of Winchester.)

'Southampton Town Wall', B. H. St. J. O'Neil, in *Aspects of Archaeology*, ed. by W. F. Grimes, (Essays presented to O. G. S. Crawford, H. W. Edwards, 1951).

VIII

The Medieval Countryside

AGRICULTURE has for long been the staple industry of Hampshire and its development, from the time of the Norman Conquest onwards, has been largely determined by the varying physical characteristics of differing parts of the county. A very large area is covered by downland, with much thin, poor chalky soil, land eminently suitable for sheep-grazing. The valleys of the many Hampshire rivers are more fertile and can be very productive when water meadows are properly irrigated. Much of the soil of the New Forest area is poor and gravelly and quite unsuitable for grain-growing. According to William Cobbett some of the best and earliest corn grown in England had long been raised at the foot of Portsdown Hill, but in medieval Hampshire there was little initiative to produce a high-quality agricultural crop of any kind; some of the best products probably came from a kind of model farm run by the Priory of St. Swithun's at Silkstead.

The method by which medieval Hampshire was farmed can conveniently be called the 'manorial system', but it must again be said that there was no real system and no real measure of uniformity; a 'manor' was sometimes a single house, large or small, sometimes a small village or hamlet, sometimes a very large area of land like the manors of Chilcomb, or Crondall. The amount of land in a manor varied considerably. The divisions of the county into 'manors' is convenient, and it is followed by the *Victoria County History*, which describes Hampshire in terms of Hundreds, each Hundred being made up by many manors. Though it is dangerous to generalize, it can be said that the chief characteristics of medieval farming were the very large fields, large and unenclosed, in which every man had a holding the size of which depended on his status in the community. All the land be-longed to the manorial overlord, and the lord's own holding, worked on his behalf by his tenants, and for his benefit, was said to be 'in demesne'. There is some evidence that about half of Hampshire retained a primitive two-field system of crop rotation until the thirteenth century when three open fields became more usual. Open fields were not so frequently found on either side of Southampton Water where there was much marsh and forest land, but even marsh and forest land was often subject to the same proportional use by peasants living near by. The varieties of soil and elevation did not make for uniformity in farming methods, but there is no doubt that much of Hampshire was not suitable for the primitive arable farming methods of the Middle Ages, and it has been suggested that real arable strip farming was only to be found in very limited areas in the county.

Villages were small and had few permanent buildings for there was no easily worked local stone. Considerable use was also made of another traditional and local building material, chalk, which could be easily quarried out of the sides of hills and downs, and was used for walls, for making coffins, and occasionally as at Selborne Priory, for substantial medieval building. When stone was used, it was nearly always brought *via* Southampton from Binsted in the Isle of Wight, from Beer in Devon, or from Caen in Normandy. Certain important buildings were roofed in large tiles made of slate from the west country, and slate also formed an important part of Southampton's coastal trade. Encaustic (decorated) tiles were often used to cover the floors of many churches and monastic buildings, and much use was made of Hampshire's cheapest building material, the flint which could be so easily gathered from fields by cheap and hard labour. Large

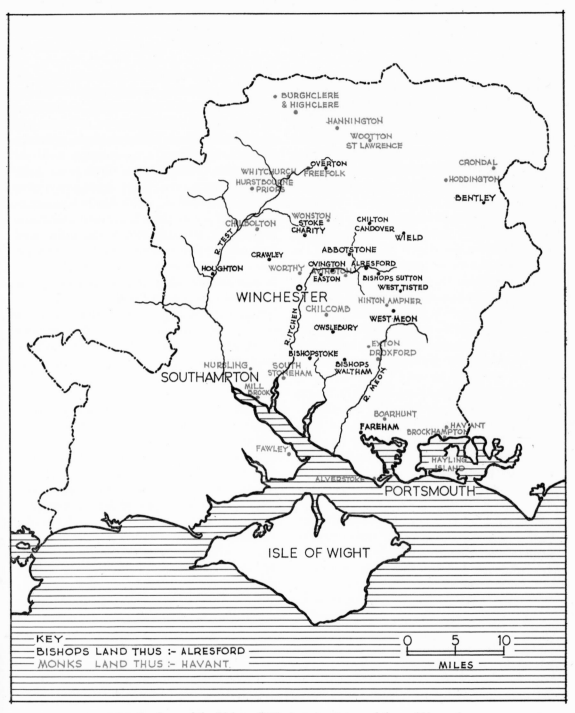

Map 6. Some of the Bishop of Winchester's estates and those of his monks.

private houses in the county, whether manors, castles or farms were usually built of a mixture of stone and flint, but in contrast to great dwellings, the average Hampshire peasant lived in a modest cottage-hut of wattle and daub, with a roof of straw or reed thatch which often caught fire. Amongst larger medieval county houses which survive in part today, much of the walling of the episcopal palace at Bishop's Waltham is of flint; the Courthouse at East Meon (which has windows and a roof which appears to date from the fourteenth century) has a stone fireplace and a stone corbelled head said to be a portrait of King John, at Warnford the ruined stone hall-house of the de Port family is of exceptional interest.

A general survey of Hampshire agriculture in the Middle Ages before the Black Death is not possible, but surviving records do give a clear picture of certain rural communities. At Highclere, in the north of the county, the bishop's manor house was a great mansion with many outbuildings, including granges for wood and logs, a dovecot and a brewery. The house was the *caput*, that is the centre of a large area including Burghclere and Ecchinswell. The farm grew many kinds of crops, barley, oats, peas and vetches, but its chief product was wool from the many sheep grazing in the valley between Beacon Hill and Sidown Range. Italian merchants bought this wool, and Englishmen, including the famous Simon the Draper of Winchester. Farther south, at Crawley, there is much to be learnt of how the open field system worked in Hampshire. In both north and south Crawley there were three great open fields, each used for a rotation of crops which seems to have been first fallow when the beasts were turned on to the land, then winter grain followed by spring grain. Most of the hard work of Hampshire farming was done by villeins who had to work the demesne land for their lord as well as look after their own strip-plots. In many areas, the proportion of free tenants to villeins was small. At Compton, a manor belonging to

the Priory of St. Swithun, there were only four free tenants in 1287: one of them was the reeve of the village who paid a rent including a measure of strawberries to be delivered each year to the Infirmary of the Priory. At Morestead the most prominent free tenant was Bernard le Moyne who had to provide the priory with five hundred and fifty eggs at Christmas and two-thirds of a bushel of strawberries on St. John's Day. His holding can be identified with the present Old Down Farm. At Silkstead the Priory kept a model farm served by a permanent resident staff, and here the priors often spent a summer holiday. Grapes were grown regularly in the vineyards at Silkstead, peafowl bred for the table, and a great pigeon house built in 1307 provided a welcome addition to plain winter fare.

Just as the manors varied in acreage, so too the holdings held by individual tenants differed enormously in size and in productivity. In the village of Yateley a number of priory tenants held virgates of land, but the virgate varied in size from twelve and a half acres upwards; all over Hampshire holdings passed from father to son, or from a tenant to his widow simply by the immemorial custom of each manor, declared in the manor court, and made valid by the payment of fine (a fee usually paid in goods or services) to the lord. Manorial lords thus had several sources of revenue, and potential capital resources, rents, profits from sale of surplus product, and the fines of their courts.

The life of every village was regulated by the custom of the manor to which it belonged, and this regulation was carried out by the manorial court which met regularly, to punish infringements of the custom, and to accept new tenants for vacant holdings, a profitable procedure since every new holder of land had to pay his lord a heriot, a fine to succeed as heir, usually his best animal, or its equivalent in money. All the normal farming processes necessary to work the land were divided out amongst the lord's unfree tenants, according to the custom of the manor. The most important surviving group of these customs is contained in the custumal of St. Swithun's Priory, written down at the end of the thirteenth century and providing much information about the customs of the priory manors all over Hampshire. Men and women were required to work the lord's land at harvest time, or to send a substitute, to plough, to carry the seed from the lord's court to where it had to be sown, to help with threshing, and with the making of manure heaps. Unfree tenants, like Walter de la Lane at Swansdrop in Crondall, could neither sell a house nor an ox, nor marry off their daughters without payment of fine to the lord. At Yateley, near by, a comparatively large holding of over one hundred acres, held by Juliana de Aula, was rented by a wide variety of payments in money and in kind, four stoups of honey, two hens at Christmas, and twenty eggs at Easter, as well as services of ploughing, reaping and weeding the lord's land. Commutation, the substitution of money rents for services, only came in very slowly towards the end of the thirteenth century, and Hampshire villages were largely self-supporting, and the only essentials which had to be brought from a distance were salt and iron. There was little market gardening of fruit or vegetables for re-sale, and the chief and essential aim of medieval farming was the production of a food and drink grain crop to provide bread and beer for the farming community itself and for the manorial overlord, though obviously some supplies were grown deliberately for certain market towns. Stock raising was very hazardous indeed, animals were small, frequently ravaged by disease, and there was no incentive to careful or selective breeding, for most animals were grazed or pastured together on open or common land. The many references to fencing or enclosure often prove to be temporary arrangements, made for example at lambing time. For the average Hampshire peasant life was often harsh, short, and wearying, an existence only lightened by the holydays of the church.

One of the most interesting of all controversies affecting the economy of the medieval countryside concerns the New Forest. It used to be said that the making of the Forest was William the Conqueror's great Hampshire crime. Yet even the most detailed study of Domesday Book fails to produce evidence other than the indubitable fact that a number of holdings had been taken into the Forest by 1086 either completely or in part. There is no evidence at all from any source to suggest that the Conqueror obliterated vast numbers of towns and villages or demolished sixty churches. Much of the area has very poor soil, and it could never have sustained a large population. In prehistoric times the Forest afforded shelter, but there are only slight traces of early habitation—Beaker folk at Fordingbridge, Minstead, Lymington and Hurn; the population may have increased in the late Bronze Age, for a number of cemeteries survive from this period, and Bronze Age man and his successors all used Hengistbury Head with its many natural advantages as a Hampshire landing-place. In the Roman period the timber and brush-wood of the New Forest was used in the widely scattered kilns making greyish and red and white pottery. Even in 1100 the Forest was called Ytene, land of the Jutes, and it was probably these people whose descendants were working the few acres of good land and making a few clearings in the later Anglo-Saxon period. Forest place names ending in -ley, -wood, and -hurst, and -shaw, are indications of this kind of change. Cnut fined those who hunted his Forest illegally, but in the early medieval period Forest law was much more severe; death and mutilation were the penalties, and the royal hunter's course was unimpeded, for until 1483 it was illegal to make any kind of enclosure for the protection of young trees or of animals. Some of the inhabitants, however, did benefit by 'Commoner's Rights', the privilege of turning out livestock to graze in the Forest at certain periods. Instead of the normal kind of manorial court found in other parts of Hampshire, Courts of Regard,

Attachment and Swainmote dealt with human and with canine offenders against Forest Laws, and special Justices visited the area regularly to punish the most serious infringements.

Stone was even more infrequently used for building in the New Forest than it was in other parts of Hampshire countryside. A mixture of heather and clay produced walls of 'cob', the usual material of domestic buildings, stone being reserved for churches, and for the great Cistercian abbey of Beaulieu, the Forest's most important medieval building.

Further reading: 'Field-system and Enclosures in Hampshire', W. E. Tate, (H.F.C. *Proceedings* XVI Pt. 3).

'Four centuries of Farming Systems in Hampshire', G. E. Fussell, (H.F.C. *Proceedings*, XVII Pt. 3).

Compton, J. S. Drew (Warren & Son, 1959).

The Economic and Social History of an English Village (Crawley), W. C. B. and E. C. Gras (Harvard, 1930).

Pages from the History of Highclere, G. D. Dunlop (Holywell Press, 1940).

The New Forest; A Symposium (Galley Press, 1960).

New Forest (H. M. Stationery Office, 1961).

IX

Hampshire During the Black Death and the Hundred Years War 1337–1444

THE great dynastic struggle between the rival houses of France and England which began in 1337, lasted for more than the hundred years which gave it its name. It was a period of great change in Hampshire, of social unrest, of major economic trouble, and problems of decline in population. The county was vulnerable to attacks from France and her allies, and the wool trade suffered from the vicissitudes of war. Men were called away from the land and before long the Black Death seriously upset the economy of a county unused to rapid social change. The Black Death may have resulted in a violent break up of the manorial system but it has also been suggested that it was merely part of the pattern of what can be called normal medieval catastrophe, of recurring plague on mankind, murrain on sheep, famine and the devastations of war. Hampshire suffered in the great European famine of 1315–17, and Hampshire farms lying on the route of men marching to war were always dangerously situated. The reeve at Silkstead paid fairly large and regular sums in bribes to prevent his stock being harmed or his corn carts taken for military transport.

In October, 1348, the Bishop of Winchester, Edington, who had already received news of the Black Death and of its dreadful effects on the Continent, issued special directions for prayers and processions for the monks of his Cathedral Church for he was 'struck with the great fear lest, which God forbid, the foul disease ravage any part of our city and diocese'. The plague was already in Dorset, and by the turn of the winter of 1348 and 1349, it was at its height in Hampshire. Though this initial outbreak diminished by the end of 1349, there were further severe outbreaks in 1361–2, 1369 and 1379. All the available evidence suggests that the plague of 1348–9 shook the agrarian economy of much of Hampshire and it certainly devastated Winchester. Amongst the farms belonging to Titchfield Priory there was a high mortality on the coast, at Titchfield itself in particular, but a high death rate is also indicated in certain inland areas, in Burghclere and Highclere; for example as late as 1376 at Highclere, of 103 ploughing services due only 15 were actually performed and in Burghclere the proportion was 207 to 54. In central Hampshire, the earliest record surviving for Silkstead after the first outbreaks of plague shows a considerable diminution in the numbers of cattle, sheep and pigs, and fewer people to look after the stock; there were vacant buildings at Compton which were not let again fully for as long as twenty years after 1349, fifteen families died out completely, and by 1352 the most important freeman had to mortgage his property to a London merchant. Some villages were practically wiped out, especially if they suffered in a later outbreak; thus by 1362, most of the Morestead village houses were in ruins. Manorial lords found it often difficult to find tenants, though this was not the case with many of the Titchfield holdings, which were at least nominally filled, though sometimes apparently by mere children. The Isle of Wight is said to have been virtually depopulated; Brading sea mill was vacant in 1349 for 'no Miller would come because of the mortality'; the average number of *Inquisitiones post mortem*, in the Island (inquiries after death concerning the property of notable persons) was one a year, but in 1349 there were seven deaths thus recorded, all people of considerable local importance. There is no doubt, either, that there was a very high death rate amongst the clergy all over the county; the high mortality is referred to in Bishop Edington's register in an entry of 14th January, 1348-9, and for that year, out of a total of some eighty-three livings vacant, thirty at least were caused by death. Amongst those who died were the incumbents of Farnham, Wallop, Hurstbourne, Abbot's Ann, Greatham, South Tidworth, Crondall, Amport and Basingstoke, as well as the Prior of Christchurch and St. Swithun's and the Abbess of St. Mary's, Winchester. In the first three months of 1349 there were at least six vacant livings caused by death in the city of Winchester and many churches fell into disuse, amongst them St. Lawrence in the very heart of Winchester, where the Rector was allowed to find another living because of the ruin of his parish. It was necessary for Bishop William of Wykeham to threaten to excommunicate laymen who dismantled churches or usurped their sites and in 1376 the mayor and bailiffs of Winchester were actually cited to appear in the cathedral before the bishop for illegally taking the sites of St. Petroc, St. Martin in the Wall and St. Nicholas. Many years after, Winchester was said to be in such a state of economic decline that there were in 1452 nearly a thousand houses empty or in ruins, and seventeen parish churches inofficiate. The decline was definite but it was only in part a result of the Black Death, other factors being the difficulties of the woollen cloth industry, and the restrictive regulations of the Corporation which drove men to live anywhere rather than within the walls of Winchester, regulations which in fact helped to produce a revolt in 1381 against the city's burgher oligarchy.

The centre of Winchester before 1348 was tightly packed and disease spread rapidly. Even though the town had the advantage of many streams and brooks running through it and two large public lavatories, the only conduited water supply was for the monks of the cathedral, and the townspeople took their water from the brooks and from wells including the common city well near the High Cross. From the early years of Edward I's reign, in contrast, the townspeople of Southampton had a good water supply, thanks to the grant to the town of a conduit house and piped water supply by the Friars Minor. Perhaps on the whole Southampton was healthier and less cramped than Winchester, but in 1338 the town was sacked by the French and much of it had to be rebuilt. Though the townspeople had been given numerous murage grants to complete the walling, in fact the work had not been carried out. It was feared that the French might return, trade suffered and some merchants moved to Bristol. The Black Death was a further blow and by the last quarter of the fourteenth century, the population of Southampton has been calculated as less than two thousand. A period of security and revived trade followed the temporary peace with France in 1389, and the presence of many Italian merchants was a very important factor in the prosperity of late medieval Southampton, when colonies of Venetian and Genoese traders and other Italian merchants from Florence and Milan helped to make the town a cosmopolitan centre. The greater part of Southampton's varied imports was distributed through Bargate by carriers to many parts of southern England. In the reign of Henry V the King's attempts to create a Royal Navy were centred on Southampton, for it was a Southampton draper and general contractor, William Soper, whose father had been a Winchester merchant, who constructed several of Henry's most important ships including the *Grace Dieu*, the largest ship to be built in England before 1637. War thus brought a temporary prosperity to Southampton, but Henry VI's advisers sold most of the Royal Navy by auction in 1422, and Southampton was never again a likely centre for naval development.

Thus the years of the Hundred Years' War were years of difficulty and decline for Hampshire towns, though decline was sometimes temporarily camouflaged by the false pros-

11. Alice Cowdreye, a nun of Wherwell, *c.* 1520, and sister of Peter Cowdreye, of Herriard. From the original painting at Herriard Park, reproduced by kind permission of J. L. Jervoise, Esq.

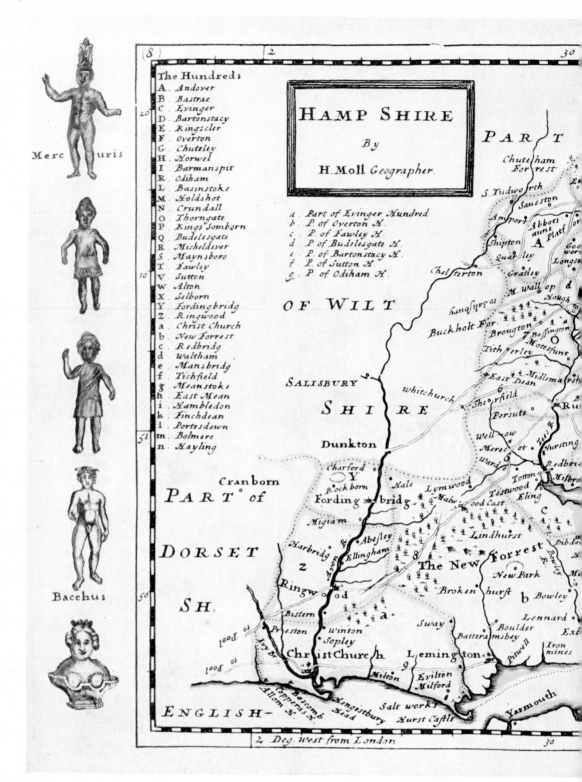

The Hundreds
A. Andover
B. Bastrae
C. Evinger
D. Bartonstacy
E. Kingseler
F. Overton
G. Chuteley
H. Horwel
I. Barmanspit
K. Odiham
L. Basinstoke
M. Holdshot
N. Crundall
O. Thorngate
P. Kings Somborn
Q. Budelesgate
R. Micheldever
S. Maynsboro
T. Fawley
V. Sutton
W. Alton
X. Selborn
Y. Fordingbridg
Z. Ringwood
a. Christ Church
b. New Forrest
c. Redbridg
d. Waltham
e. Mansbridg
f. Tichfield
g. Meanstoke
h. East Mean
i. Hambledon
k. Finchdean
l. Portesdown
m. Bolmere
n. Hayling

a . Part of Evinger Hundred
b . P. of Overton H .
c . P. of Fawley H .
d . P. of Budelesgate H .
e . P. of Bartonstacy H .
f . P. of Sutton H .
g . P. of Odiham H .

HAMP SHIRE
By
H. Moll Geographer.

Mercurius

Bacchus

12. Hampshire by Herman Moll, from

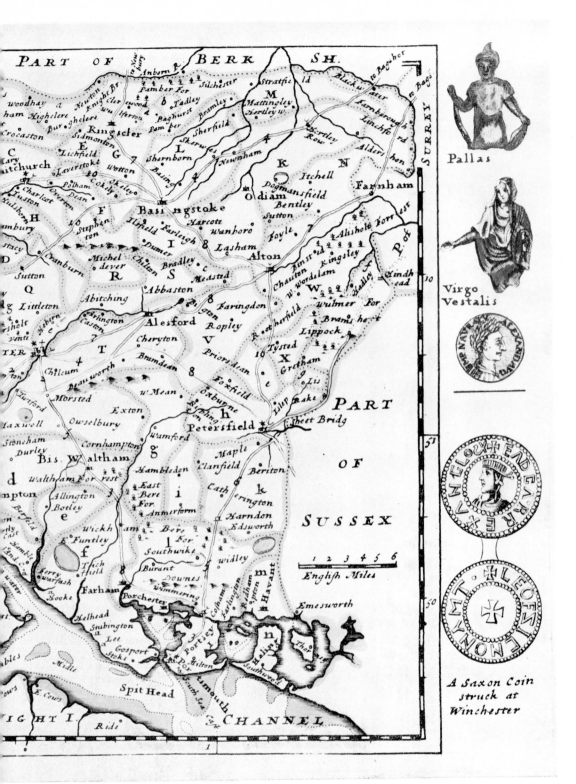

Pallas

Virgo Vestalis

A Saxon Coin struck at Winchester

A Description of England and Wales, 1724.

13. The Vyne at Sherborne St. John, near Basingstoke: the western façade.

14. Effigy of Sir Thomas Wriothesley (1505–1550), 1st Baron Wriothesley of Titchfield and Earl of Southampton, on his tomb in Titchfield Church.

Map 7. Internal Trade in late medieval Hampshire.

perity brought about by the bustle of war and the individual fortunes made by contractors like Soper in Southampton and by innkeepers such as Mark le Faire in Winchester. In the county generally there was recovery, but a definite decline in population, and the process of change by which money rents were paid instead of services given, was accentuated. More and more demesne land was farmed out for a paid rent by lords who could not otherwise get their land worked at all; on some manors the large common fields decreased in size and some were eventually cut up. Yet it was not mere economic and social change which was to prove the most important sign of the end of the Middle Ages. The brutali-ties of war, and the horrors of the Black Death, shook men's faith and belief in the teaching of the Church. It was not always easy to believe in the resurrection of the body or the sacredness of human life; the re-building of much of Winchester Cathedral begun by Bishop Edington and completed by William of Wykeham stands as a great act of faith in a world of increasing religious difficulties and of declining moral values.

Further reading : Southampton Essays, 1958 : 'Southampton as a Naval Centre, 1414–1458', Barbara Carpenter Turner.
Register of William of Wykeham, ed. T. F. Kirby (Hants Record Society, 2 Vols, 1896, 1899).

X

The Diocese of Winchester before the Reformation

RELIGIOUS life in medieval Hampshire owed much to the dedicated men and women whose lives were spent within the walls of monasteries and convents. After the Norman Conquest, the number of monastic houses increased and to the older Benedictine communities of nuns at St. Mary's Winchester, Wherwell and Romsey, of monks at Newminster and Old Minster in Winchester, were added Cistercian monasteries at Quarr (Isle of Wight) (c. 1132), Beaulieu (1204) and Netley (1239), a small Cistercian nunnery at Wintney (before 1200) as well as other quasi-monastic establishments of canons following the Rule of St. Augustine. The Cistercians, whose order was named from the parent house of Citeaux in Burgundy and whose greatest member in medieval Christendom was St. Bernard of Clairvaux, were fundamentally not a new order of monks but a severe and rigidly reformed community following the Benedictine rule with simplicity on secluded sites away from wordly distractions. Manual labour was an important part of their daily life and each house had its own *Conversi*, lay brethren who were not likely to become monks but were a second order occupied in much hard manual work. There was thus many opportunities within each Cistercian house for men and women who were not of the intellectual standard associated with Benedictine monasteries. Unlike the Benedictines, however, Cistercian foundations were not great feudal landowners, and their income was largely derived from their own physical efforts. Sheep-farming and forestry were the chief occupations of the monks at Netley and Beaulieu. Both Cistercians and Benedictine monks were 'regulars', that is real monks following a definite 'rule', *regula*. Another kind of ecclesiastical foundation was that provided by the houses of canons, secular priests following the so-called rule of St. Augustine, who lived a communal life in their houses at Breamore (founded c. 1128–33), Portchester (1133), which later moved to Southwick (1145–53), St. Denys, Southampton (1127), Christchurch (c. 1150), Mottisfont (1201) and Selborne (1233). An additional house of canons of the order of Prémontre was founded at Titchfield in c. 1232, whose inhabitants, 'white' canons, to distinguish them from the 'black' canons of the order of St. Augustine, did much the same sort of religious work, preaching as missionaries, acting as parish priests, and devoting a large part of their time, at least in the early years of their houses, to manual labour on their estates.

Of other religious houses, only the Benedictines were subject to episcopal control by visitations and subsequent injunctions, and medieval bishops often found it necessary to inquire into, control and reform the houses under their care. Bishops of Winchester have had a particular relationship with their own cathedral Benedictine priory, being elected by the Prior and his monks (acting as the Dean and Chapter); a tradition which in theory remains unbroken today. Once elected, the relationship between the monks and the bishop was almost that of a monastery with its abbot, and the cathedral fabric as it is today is almost entirely the work of a series of changes instituted and paid for by successive diocesan bishops.

The first Norman bishop, a friend of William Rufus, Walkelin (1070–98) rebuilt the cathedral entirely and pulled down the Old Minster. He also seems to have built himself a palace at East Meon. William Giffard (1107–29) was the first of many Winchester bishops to be also Chancellors of England, and was one of the earliest of the English bishops to recognize the Cistercian revival of monasticism, by the foundation just over the Hampshire border (but in the diocese) of Waverley Abbey in 1128. His successor, Henry de Blois, 1129–71, was an outstanding bishop in every way. A Cluniac monk, and brother of that Stephen, who was one of the claimants to the English throne after the death of Henry I in 1135, his early career was that of a politician and scholar rather than that of an ecclesiastic. As well as being Bishop of Winchester he was also Abbot of Glastonbury which he readorned and enriched with great generosity from a vast private fortune. This fortune also enabled him to give munificently to Winchester Cathedral and to found the most famous almshouse in the kingdom, the Hospital of the Holy Cross at Sparkford, better known as St. Cross. His ambitions were unbounded; he was actually elected Archbishop of Canterbury in 1136 and when his enemies in Rome prevented the Pope from confirming the election, de Blois got himself made Papal Legate in England, with precedence over the Archbishop of Canterbury. Later on, he tried— but in vain—to have Winchester made into an archbishopric and in the south-eastern corner of the city built a great episcopal palace, Wolvesey. He constructed other great fortified castle residences at Merdon, Farnham and Bishop's Waltham, valuable military strongholds for a bishop actively engaged in civil war. At the accession of Henry II in 1154, de Blois went into exile, back to his old monastery at Cluny, whence he returned about three years later, a reformed character, a benevolent elder statesman, and the senior English bishop. Though as Chancellor, Thomas Becket had helped to demolish de Blois' castles, the Bishop supported Thomas as Archbishop in his struggle with Henry II, and he died in 1171, a venerable and beloved statesman. De Blois' episcopate is contemporary with that great artistic revival known as the Romanesque renaissance of the twelfth century, a revival exemplified by a severe and dignified architectural style, by carving in ivory, by sumptuous metal and enamel work, by richly embossed bookbinding, and by a style of manuscript illumination which reached its greatest beauty and power in the Latin Vulgate known as the Winchester Bible.

The revenues of the medieval bishopric were in fact so large that it was difficult for medieval bishops of Winchester not to be generous. A large proportion of the bishop's income came from his many and scattered Hampshire estates; some of this income was in money, a proportion was in goods in kind, either used directly by the bishop and his household when he stayed in the district, or sent by local officials whenever required. All the many local officials kept detailed accounts compiled eventually into a great series of records known as the Bishop of Winchester's Pipe Rolls, a wonderful series, beginning in 1208 which provide a detailed and complete account of the manorial estates of the Bishops of Winchester. The records were kept as rolls till 1454; after that date they continue as folios and though not every manor is mentioned individually every time, the general picture is complete and provides a fascinating story of a great feudal itinerant household with a central treasury under a steward or seneschal at Wolvesey, Winchester. Some bishops had the help of a suffragan or of an assistant bishop and indeed this was apparently quite usual in the fourteenth century. Suffragans were usually bishops '*in partibus*', that is to say bishops with foreign titles, for example Peter Corbaviensis (1322–31), William Salubiensis (1407–1417), or they were Irish diocesan bishops acting in England; one suffragan, Caesarius de Rosis (1349–55) is said to have been a Franciscan. Much of the routine work of the diocese was carried out by the Archdeacons of Surrey and of Winchester. The usual form of address for an archdeacon was simply Dominus, and the use of 'Venerable' did not apparently appear persistently in the Winchester diocese until after 1802. It was the archdeacon's duty, on receipt of a mandate from the bishop, to induct the clerics appointed to vacant livings, and sometimes he carried out the Induction in person and sometimes by deputy. Another essential part of diocesan organization was the procedure for proving wills, which had to be proved before officials of the bishop or of the archdeacons, unless they were made by people living in a limited number of districts called 'Peculiars', having their own procedure. Disputes about legacies or wills were dealt with by the Bishop's Consistory Court which was held in any suitable church in the early medieval period, but from about 1404 was housed in a special gallery built at the west end of the north aisle of Winchester Cathedral. The Consistory Court also dealt with matrimonial disputes, and cases which concerned the discipline of the clergy. All the various official acts of each bishop, important documents of his episcopate, visitations, notes of ordinations and inductions, were kept, and still are kept by each bishop's Registrar in a volume therefore called the Register.

The medieval diocese of Winchester was very large, and the bishops moved round it slowly in comfort and dignity when they were not engaged elsewhere as royal civil servants or politicians. It included the counties of Hampshire and of Surrey and also the present dioceses of Portsmouth and Guildford, but not the Channel Islands, which only came into the care of the Bishop of Winchester in the sixteenth century. In London, the bishop had a large palatial home, Winchester House at Southwark, as well as a prison known as the Clink, and within the diocese he had many residences.

In 1208 Bishop Peter de Roches, like all his medieval successors, had three chief seats, at Farnham, Winchester and Taunton, Somerset, and secondary residences at Waltham, Clere, Downton and Merdon, Marwell, and Bishop's Waltham. His manors at Fareham and at Bitterne (on the site of the Roman port of *Clausentum*) were centres for the essential redistribution of wine and salt. Though the accounts give much information about the economic aspect of the Bishop's political activities, they also show de Roches as the purchaser of hawks and hunting dogs, for like his King, John, the Bishop was a keen huntsman. Every bishop had a large personal retinue of cleric and of laymen, many of whom attended on him because of the work he did in his other capacities.

It is almost surprising, in fact, to find that most medieval bishops did devote so much time to the ecclesiastical duties of their diocese. Bishop John de Pontoise (or Pontissara, 1282–1304) founded a great chapel at Winchester, served by a College of secular priests, and dedicated to St. Elizabeth of Hungary, where masses were to be said daily for the souls of the Bishops of Winchester and of all the faithful. Though there were many parish churches, he seems to have begun the licensing of private chapels in manor houses, amongst them one at Tichborne for the family who were famous as the distributors of a 'dole' of flour given annually to all their village tenants, a custom which still continues. It was during Pontissara's episcopate that a great financial survey was made of the diocese by order of Pope Nicholas IV in order to provide money for the Church. This *Taxatio* shows that most parishes in Hampshire were served by priests who were rectors, though they might not be resident: there were comparatively few vicarages, and these only in benefices with large financial endowments. Yet many of the rectories were small and ill-endowed, and the life of the average parish priest was far-removed from the wealth and luxury of the diocesan bishop. Even Bishop John de Pontissara, however, had to borrow money to meet his expenditure when on royal business at Rome. It would be pleasant to think that when he did visit his diocese he rode on the very expensive black palfrey given him by Edward I, just as Henry Woodlock, his successor (1305–1316) rode through the diocese on his palfreys Braybrook and Bereford. Woodlock loved his work and unlike most of the Bishops of Winchester, was a Hampshire man and the only Prior of St. Swithun's to become bishop.

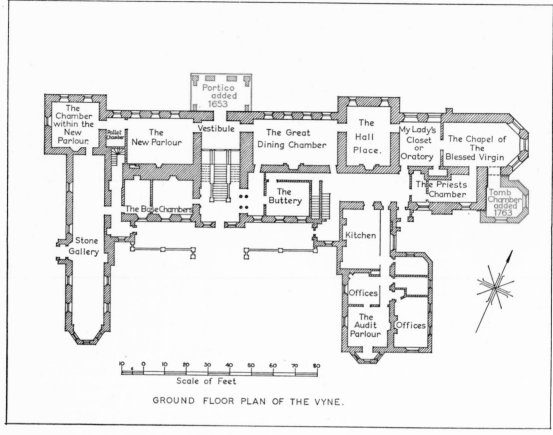

GROUND FLOOR PLAN OF THE VYNE.

Map 8.   The Vyne, ground floor, c. 1540. (See pages 52–3.)

He was not a politician, and a glance at his itinerary for only one year, 1308, will show how he spent his time in the service of his diocese. Early in 1308 he helped to crown Edward II at Westminster, and then held an ordination at St. Mary Overy, now Southwark Cathedral. In June and July he was at Marwell, Bitterne and East Meon and on Trinity Sunday ordained one hundred and twenty candidates at Southampton. By September he was at Highclere and then at Farnham for a further big ordination service. In the winter he was again in the Surrey half of the diocese, at Farnham, Esher and Southwark, but spent Christmas at Highclere. A charming letter of invitation to the Prior of St. Swithun's to keep the Christmas of 1310 with him at Wolvesey records Woodlock as

friendly and firm; the Prior was definitely to come to Wolvesey, no plea of other engagement to stand in the way.

His successor, John Sandale (1316-1319) took some action against pluralists, incumbents who held more than one living, and also against clergy who were non-resident. By visitations and injunctions he rebuked monks and nuns for breaking their rules. A young chaplain, from St. Mary's Nunnery, Winchester, strutting round Winchester in a gay parti-coloured habit, had the misfortune to meet the Bishop in person. He was severely rebuked, as was the abbess for allowing such a scandal.

The episcopate of William of Edington (1346-1366) was marred by the Black Death, yet Edington's most remembered achieve-

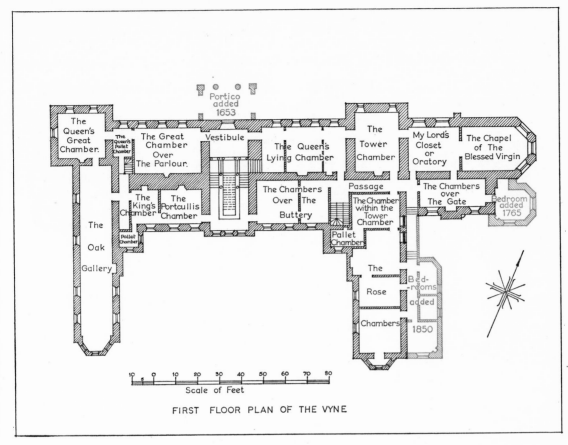

Map 9.   The Vyne, first floor, c. 1540.

ment is that he began the rebuilding of Winchester Cathedral, a task which he did not live to complete. The relations between the diocesan bishops and the Priory Church of St. Swithun in Winchester, their cathedral, has always been of great importance and the cathedral fabric, as it stands today, is almost entirely the work of the bishops of the diocese. The last of the great builders, before the Reformation, were William of Wykeham (1367–1404) and Richard Fox (1501–1528).

Both Wykeham and Fox were remarkable for the energy and time they devoted to the pressing problems of diocesan reform. Wykeham's famous foundation, St. Mary College of Winchester, was founded in 1382 and was designed for seventy poor scholars, its object being to provide a sound education for

men who were likely to go into the church. Repeated injunctions in his register reflect the low standard of clerical learning; thus, in 1385, he ordered the Rector of St. Michael's in Jewry Street, Winchester to learn by heart the Creed, the Ten Commandments and 'other things which a Minister ought to know'; an injunction which indicates a lack of elementary standards for a cleric in a cathedral city. There were, however, far too many churches in medieval Winchester for their respective parishes to survive the depletion of the city at the time of the Black Death. Bishop Fox greatly reduced the number by uniting certain livings, and long before his time the problem of church work in the poorer districts and outskirts of Winchester was partly solved by the coming of the Friars,

47

and the erection of four great friary churches. Until the Black Death there were probably never less than sixty active parish churches in Winchester, a great contrast with Portsmouth and Southampton.

Further reading: The Churches of Medieval Winchester, Barbara Carpenter Turner (Warren & Son, 1957).
Hampshire Inductions, ed. F. T. Madge (Warren & Son, 1918).
A History of Winchester College, A. F. Leach (Duckworth, 1899).

Winchester Cathedral Cartulary, ed. A. F. Goodman (Warren & Son, 1927).
The Winchester Bible, W. F. Oakeshott (Faber & Faber, 1945).
The Episcopal Colleagues of Thomas Becket, David Knowles (C.U.P., 1951).
The Muniments of the Bishopric of Winchester, C. Deedes (1912).
Register of John De Pontissara, ed. C. Deedes (Canterbury and York Society, 1915).
Register of Henry de Woodlock, ed. A. W. Goodman (Canterbury and York Society, 1941).
Register of William of Wykeham, ed. T. F. Kirby (Hampshire Record Society, 2 Vols, 1896, 1899).

15. Bere Mill on the River Test where Henri de Portal first made paper in 1712.

16. Distribution of the Dole by Sir Henry Tichborne at Tichborne Manor, in 1670. From the painting by Gillis van Tilborch, by kind permission of Sir Anthony Tichborne, Bt.

17. Basingstoke in *c.* 1840. From Robert Mudie's *History of Hampshire*.

18. The Pier at Bournemouth, *c.* 1875.

XI

The Reformation in Hampshire

DURING the greater part of the sixteenth century the minds of Hampshire men and women were troubled and perplexed by the many religious changes of the times, changes of the Reformation and Counter-Reformation, which eventually led to the establishment of a national Anglican Church with the Sovereign at its head, a Church claiming to be Catholic in doctrine but independent of papal authority. The monasteries were the last possible bastion of papal supremacy in England and for this reason, as well as for other political and financial motives, Henry VIII decided to close them.

In some ways, it is the dissolution of the Hampshire monasteries which marks the end of the Middle Ages in Hampshire. Yet it would be a mistake to think that 'Reform' only began in the reign of Henry VIII. Many of the later medieval bishops had shown a keen and informed interest in diocesan affairs. Wykeham's attempts to provide for the education of his clergy led him to found, not a monastery, but two colleges, one at Winchester for boys, the other at New College for undergraduates. The problems of small or inefficient monasteries were noticed long before 1536, and there was a plan to close Mottisfont as early as 1494 which was not proceeded with, though Bishop Waynflete (1447–86) did close Selborne Priory, and used its endowments for his new collegiate foundation of Magdalen College, Oxford. Fox's episcopate (1501–28) was marked by careful and moderate reform, for he instituted the now familiar policy of unifying small benefices in towns, closing redundant churches, and he also completed the work of Edington and Wykeham in the cathedral by improving the choir and giving it a beautiful new wooden vault decorated with carved and coloured bosses. His sympathy towards the new learning of the Renaissance was shown by his foundation of Corpus Christi College, Oxford, and it is significant that he, Wykeham and Waynflete all founded colleges at Oxford, not monasteries in their own diocese. Fox died in 1528, and was succeeded by Cardinal Wolsey, whose tenure of the bishopric was very brief, for he was enthroned by proxy, never held any ordinations and died in 1530. Ecclesiastical appointments made at this time suggest a definite policy of promoting those who were supporters of the Government. John Salcot, made Abbot of Hyde, surrendered his abbey at the Dissolution in return for higher office. Anne Boleyn's uncle, William Boleyn, was made Archdeacon of Winchester in January, 1530.

The main story of the first half of the Reformation in Hampshire coincides with the episcopate of Bishop Stephen Gardiner, a long period, 1531 till 1555, broken by Gardiner's suspension and imprisonment by the extreme Protestant Government of Edward VI, when the bishopric was held by a Protestant reformer, John Poynet. During Poynet's episcopate an arrangement was made with the Crown by which the Bishop received a fixed annual revenue in return for the surrender of his lands, but this plan, by which not only the Crown but also the Marquess of Winchester appears to have benefited, was apparently cancelled in the reign of Mary, and the bishops kept their estates till the middle of the nineteenth century. Yet there is little in the registers of either Gardiner and Poynet to suggest that this was a time when men were giving their lives for their religious beliefs, and nothing at all to show the doctrinal changes or the reactions of Hampshire men to them. The dissolution of the Hampshire monasteries is hardly apparent at all in Gardiner's Register but a detailed account of the various houses was, however, compiled in 1501 by Dr. Thomas Hede when he conducted a visitation of the monasteries at a time when both the sees of Winchester and of Canterbury were vacant.

Hede began his inspection at St. Swithun, Winchester. He found only thirty-five monks, but nothing to complain of there, or in the other Winchester houses of St. Mary's and Hyde. All the other Hampshire houses were satisfactory, with the exception of St. Denys, Southampton, where one piece of church plate was in pawn, and Romsey where convent life had obviously become almost a farce. A little later on, in 1533, Wherwell Abbey became notorious for a brief while because of the behaviour of its Abbess, Anne Colt, but this was an exceptional case; the previous Abbess, Alice Cowdreye was said to have been 'pleasant to God and true to the king'. Yet in 1536 no excuse of good conduct or proper administration could save the Hampshire monasteries from the King's determination to close them and by the end of the year St. Denys, Netley and Quarr had all 'surrendered'. In 1537 Titchfield was closed, and handed over to Thomas Wriothesley who converted the fabric of the church into a great private house. Beaulieu fell to his lot also in 1538, as did Southwick which eventually passed to one of his servants, John White. At Hyde, Winchester, Wriothesley used the monastery as a stone quarry for his new house at Titchfield, and the complaisant abbot was made Bishop of Salisbury. At St. Swithun's, Winchester, Wriothesley, accompanied by his fellow commissioners Pollard and Williams, and by the Mayor of Winchester, and some of the Corporation's 'best brethren' destroyed the great shrine of the patron saint in the middle of the night of September, 1538, for fear of the citizens' disapproval. Yet the cathedral survived, the capitular body was reformed as a Dean and Chapter, and the last prior, William Kingsmill, became the first Dean. At St. Mary's, Winchester the last abbess, Elizabeth Shelley, surrendered her abbey, retired on a pension as did the majority of monks and nuns, and

continued to live a quasi-conventual life in Winchester with a group of nuns from the abbey.

Sweeping as these changes were, much of the old doctrine of the Catholic Church remained as before, and it was not until the reign of Edward VI that the real effect of reform was felt. A new liturgy, in English, contained in two successive Prayer Books superseded the old Latin missal, and liturgical books were thrown away, sold as scrap, or used as covers for the new church parish registers of baptisms, burials and marriages which Thomas Cromwell had ordered every incumbent to keep from 1538 onwards. To quote only a few examples, at St. Michael's, Southampton, and at Southwick, the earliest parish registers are bound in parts of fifteenth-century missals, at Greatham, a late medieval Gradual serves as cover, and there are fragments of pre-Reformation theological bindings similarly used on registers at Brockenhurst and Micheldever. In 1550 the church-wardens of St. John, Winchester, sold a hundredweight of old parchment books for six shillings, pieces of alabaster for one shilling and fourpence, and a 'guilded image' for only a shilling, though in 1551–54 they sold a cross and a chalice for the very large sum of £22 17s. 10d. At the beginning of Mary's reign, Bishop Gardiner was released from the Tower, and it was he who officiated at Mary's wedding to Philip of Spain in Winchester Cathedral. The reaction against extreme Protestantism is shown in his resumed register, which records that a number of Hampshire clerics were deprived of their livings, clearly men who had married or those who had accepted the Protestant Prayer Books.

The Dissolution of the Monasteries was inevitably followed by the appearance of a new class of landlord in Hampshire. Not all these 'new' men were Protestant reformers; those who kept the old faith included William Laurens of Winchester, a lawyer, who paid for the restoration of the High Cross on the occasion of the marriage of Philip and Mary in Winchester Cathedral, but who had nego-

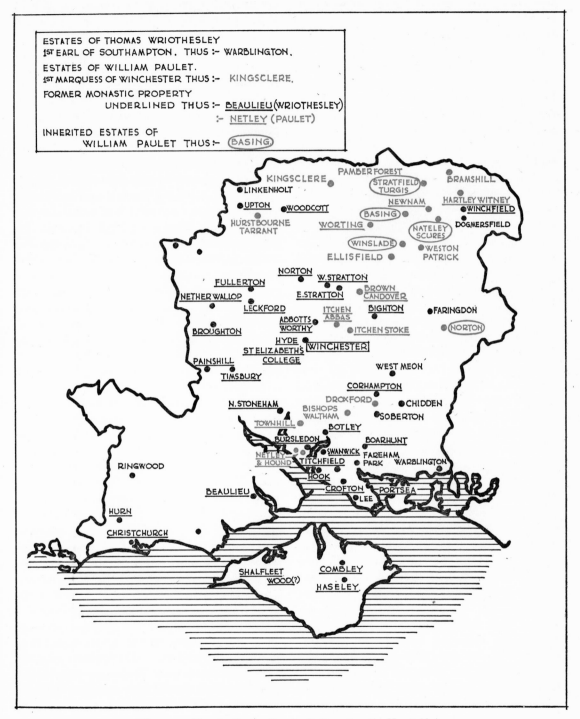

Map 10.   New landlords after the Reformation (in Hampshire).

tiated the royal charter giving the corporation the Winchester rents of some of the dissolved monasteries, a service for which he was rewarded by favourable leases of city property. Other new landlords profited on a much larger scale, Thomas Wriothesley (d. 1550) who became Earl of Southampton, has already been mentioned and perhaps profited more from the Reformation than any other man. In Southampton itself the Mille family who had acted as lawyers and stewards for the Priory of St. Swithun, and perhaps also for the Priory of Breamore, acquired more town property as well as a large estate on the western side of Southampton Water. John Mille (? 1509–1551) was Town Clerk and Recorder, and the ancestor of a well-known Hampshire family, the Barker Mills, whose property came to include the manors of Eling, Millbrook, Langley, Colbury, and Mottisfont. Typical also of the new men of the Reformation was the first Marquess of Winchester, William Paulet (d. 1572), whose great estate in Hampshire was widespread, although partly as the result of inheritance from the de Port family, including the great house at Basing soon to be the centre of Royalist resistance in the Civil War of Charles I's time. All the new Tudor landlords were in fact bound by the most practical considerations to be obedient to the monarch, and therefore to the Protestant Reformation. The first Marquess of Winchester, when asked how he survived the various political and religious changes of each reign replied that he had been a willow and not an oak. It is arguable as to how much economic change the new landlords brought to the county. There was economic distress and unemployment in late sixteenth-century Hampshire, but these were results of many factors, not just of the Reformation and the dissolution of the monasteries. The breakdown of the old system of training in craft gilds, the increased number of industrial capitalists, which made it hard for a man to set up on his own, and the numbers of soldiers and sailors returning from the wars all pro-

duced social difficulties, which were accentuated by inflation. The Government relied on Justices of the Peace to deal with unemployed and vagrant men and women, and in 1578 a large 'House of Correction' was set up for the county in Winchester, under the supervision of the County Magistrates, to provide training and supervision for all whom they sent there. In some parts of England the Reformation resulted in the enclosure of much land and a tendency to change from arable to sheep farming. Hampshire was already predominantly a sheep county, and the enclosure movement had begun before the Reformation according to Wolsey's commission of 1517, south Hampshire being enclosed earlier than the rest of the county. The greatest single example of enclosure in 1517 was of one hundred and twenty acres at Bramshill where, about one hundred years later, one of Hampshire's great country houses was built, in brick, material whose rediscovery did much to affect the architectural appearance of the county. Grove Place, at Nursling near Southampton, also in brick, was built at the end of the sixteenth century by the son of a London merchant who had profited by the Reformation, and has a formal garden of typical Tudor design.

The county's most famous house, The Vyne at Sherborne St. John, belongs to the early Tudor period and was built by the first Lord Sandys, in diapered red brick with stone ornamentation and sculptured coats of arms of Henry VIII and Catherine of Aragon and the owner himself, who was perhaps noticed by Anne Boleyn when she visited The Vyne with the King in October, 1535. Lord Sandys was a member of an ancient Hampshire family, a loyal subject of the King and not greatly involved in the religious changes of the time. An inventory of The Vyne made after his death in 1541 provides a fascinating account of the household of a great Hampshire nobleman of the period, describing each room, its contents, Lord Sandys' horses, his household linen, his jewels and his plate, as well as the contents of his personal wardrobe. His support of the ancient faith did not, however, prevent him from converting Mottisfont Priory into a secondary residence. A later member of the Sandys family entertained Elizabeth I at The Vyne in 1569, with much difficulty and great expense.

By this time, the Anglican Church settlement was more or less established but the extreme Protestant policy of Bishop Horne (1561–80) provoked much bitterness in a diocese which had been comparatively undisturbed by the Marian persecutions, and which had produced only one martyr, the Archdeacon of Winchester, John Philpot of Compton who was burnt at Smithfield in 1555. Horne destroyed all those parts of the cathedral fabric which seemed 'superstitious', windows of medieval glass, the surviving statues, and the great rood. He endeavoured to enforce the punishment of recusants, those Roman Catholics who would not attend the services of the established church, and many were subject to heavy nominal fines which were never in fact actually collected. The Hampshire families known to be recusants included the Cottons of Warblington, the Shelleys at Buriton, and some of the Paulets. Much more serious than non-attendance at church was the crime of denying the royal supremacy, and for this, two Hampshire men, John Slade and John Body, suffered the fate of traitors in 1583, Slade at Winchester, Body at Andover. Their deaths were undoubtedly intended as a warning, for the old religion remained strong in certain towns, particularly in Winchester. Religious difficulties, unemployment, political uncertainty and financial crises as well as fear of foreign invasion were the problems facing many men and women at the end of the sixteenth century.

Further reading: *History of The Vyne*, Chaloner W. Chute (Jacob & Johnson, Winchester, 1888).

'Field Systems and Enclosures', W. E. Tate (H.F.C. *Proceedings*, XVI, Pt. 3).

Wessex, G. Sewell (G. F. Wilson, Southampton, 1956).

The Parish Registers of the Archdeaconry of Winchester, ed. W. A. Fearon and J. F. Williams (Warren, 1909).

Winchester Consistory Court Depositions, 1561 No. 2. ed. A. J. Willis, 1960.

'Hampshire Recusants in the time of Elizabeth I', J. E. Paul (H.F.C. *Proceedings*, XII, Pt. II, 1959).

Registers of Bishops Gardiner, Poynet and White (Canterbury and York Society, 1930).

XII

Tudor Towns

THE military and naval activity of the Hundred Years War brought varying degrees of temporary prosperity to Hampshire towns. Both Portsmouth and Southampton suffered in the long wars with France when both were burnt, and the constitutional development of the former was hampered to a certain extent by Southampton's claim to consider Portsmouth a mere part of its own greater port and not an independent town. The county was not the scene of major fighting in the Wars of the Roses, yet the Tudor period which followed, was often a time of financial difficulty for some corporations, despite the individual prosperity of many townsmen. There is a marked contrast between the wealth of individuals and the general complaints of decay and financial hardship drawn up often by the very same men on behalf of their own boroughs.

Henry VII's decision to build a dry dock at Portsmouth in 1495 was a decisive factor in the town's future history. Though this dock was soon filled in, and though during the reign of Elizabeth I the harbour was used by many pirates, and there was also much secret coming and going on the part of Roman Catholic priests and recusants, and though royal interest centred on seaports nearer London or on the activities of west country seamen, Portsmouth's place in national history as a permanent home for the navy was soon established without doubt. In 1600, a royal charter from the Queen gave Portsmouth its first definite status as a corporate borough, under a mayor elected by the burgesses. Its importance as a naval centre and garrison town was shown by the fact that the grant was not in any way to prejudice the power of the Captain of Portsmouth. In 1627 Charles I confirmed all these privileges, granting the inhabitants also the right of making certain kinds of woollen cloth, an indication that the town's prosperity was not entirely bound up with the future of the Royal Navy. Law and order were maintained by the court-leet which dealt with all trading offences as well as frequent complaints of 'fray and bloodshed'. Religious life centred round the original Portsmouth parish church of St. Thomas (now the cathedral) and the Church of St. Mary at Kingston, which had belonged to Southwick Priory until its dissolution in 1539.

In contrast to Portsmouth, in the Tudor and early Stuart period, Southampton's fortunes were declining. By 1531 the Corporation there was almost bankrupt, chiefly because of the absence of foreign trade. The effect of the withdrawal of the Venetian galleys was particularly noticeable, and not until the nineteenth century did trade with the new world recreate the town's former commerical prosperity. Yet there were wealthy men in the Tudor town, chiefly 'new' men who had founded their fortunes as a result of the economic changes brought about by the Reformation. Amongst these were the Mille or Mills family, Town Clerks and Recorders, who were able to speculate in Southampton and Hampshire property and soon set themselves up as landed gentry, with a town house in the High Street and fine manor houses on the other side of Southampton Water.

The early Tudor period in Winchester was a time of financial difficulty in civic affairs. The Corporation attempted to meet this problem by obtaining a series of reductions in the fee-farm of the city and by obtaining permission for the mayor to take his oath of office locally instead of having to go to London with a retinue at the citizens' expense. A more positive and very special kind of financial help was given after the marriage of Philip and Mary in Winchester Cathedral, an event which required considerable local expenditure. A series of Letters Patent granted Winchester various reductions in the city's fee-farm and also gave the Corporation those properties in the city which had formerly belonged to certain dissolved monastic houses. Like Portsmouth, Winchester obtained its first charter of incorporation from Elizabeth I and this great charter set out Winchester's constitution as it had evolved from medieval times. Local Government under a Mayor and Corporation of Twenty-Four remained undisturbed until the Municipal Corporations Act of 1835.

The governments of Southampton, Portsmouth and Winchester were essentially plutocratic but these local men occasionally needed help from a social level higher than any they themselves could hope to reach. Thus in Portsmouth, the Corporation obtained the good services of Lord Mountjoy, Captain of the port there, in order to petition Elizabeth I for that charter granted in 1600. In Southampton, the Corporation approached Sir Francis Walsingham when they needed a friend at Court, and Walsingham was made Winchester's first High Steward for exactly the same practical consideration. A 'new' man himself, he thus succeeded to the position of a powerful local patron, similar to that enjoyed in medieval times by some of Hampshire's feudal nobility, including the bishops of the diocese and the lay Justices of Assize.

Despite certain economic difficulties, there were in fact many prosperous Hampshire townsfolk. Some could afford to build themselves fine town houses and where these survive, in a few places only, they are the best possible proof of the prosperity of Tudor Hampshire. The timber-framed building called 'Tudor House' in St. Michael's Square, Southampton, was built by Sir John Dawtrey, a royal customs official who was Sheriff of Hampshire in 1516. Wills and Inventories provide many details of other houses. In the reign of Elizabeth I, Winchester was something of a centre for medical

studies, and John Warner, dean from 1559 till 1564, had been first Regius Professor of Medicine. Doctor Thomas Bassett, who died in 1575, had a fine house with many rooms including a hall, a parlour furnished with joined table and stools, cushions of tapestry and needlework, a study containing a standing glass for a student, that is, a microscope, and a dispensary complete with still, at the back of the building. It is not certain where Bassett's house stood, but Doctor Simon Trippe who was Physician to the Dean and Chapter of Winchester till his death in 1596 had an even more elaborate and finely furnished establishment in what is now Colebrook House. Trippe was a Renaissance gentleman, educated at Oxford, Cambridge and Padua.

Occasionally large new Tudor houses encroached on what had been ancient lanes and rights of way. Thus in 1582 the construction of a great town mansion by Sir Walter Sandys, in charge of the Winchester garrison, meant the partial but permanent closing of the south end of Lower Brook Street in Winchester. At the western end of the south side of the High Street, the Bethell family entirely enclosed St. Nicholas' Lane for the same sort of purpose. The Bethells' main residence, Hyde House on the outskirts of Winchester was built in the new material, brick, and on the ancient site of Hyde Abbey which the family had eventually obtained from Wriothesley after the dissolution of the monastery.

A general use of brick, instead of wattle and daub, began to transform the appearance of many street frontages. The average house still occupied the site of its medieval predecessor, but increased space was sometimes obtained, as it is now, by building high. A town house which belonged to the Dean and Chapter of Winchester Cathedral, the old Manor of God-be-got, was thus rebuilt as one of the tallest timber-framed brick buildings in Tudor Winchester, with fine stone fireplaces. For many years part of it was occupied by Peter Symonds, a wealthy merchant who left most of his fortune to charity.

It would be wrong indeed to leave the Tudor period without a brief glimpse of the very large number of charitable bequests which are such a feature of that age, some carrying on old medieval traditions, but others, with their main emphasis on education and indicative of a concern for learning. Symonds left money for the almshouses called Christ's Hospital, and in Winchester, also, Ralph Lamb rebuilt the almshouses of St. John's Hospital. At Andover a free school was founded by John Hanson in 1571, the founder and first Headmaster both being Wykehamists. At Southampton a Grammar School was founded with money left for the purpose by William Capon who had been Rector of St. Mary's, and who died in 1550. Many townspeople were not only prosperous, but also public spirited and had a conscious civic pride, a pride expressed also in corporate improvements in the general standards of town life, sanitary conditions, street lighting for example, and a pride also expressed in the frequent and not always successful attempts to make compulsory the wearing of special gowns and hats by senior members of civic corporations.

This prosperity, of professional men, lawyers, doctors, schoolmasters, was to a certain extent a contrast with the prosperity of medieval towns, which was centred particularly on direct commercial activity and the profits of retail and wholesale trading; it was the source, not only of wealth, but of much of the opposition to the first Stuart kings of England.

Further reading : Catalogue of Historical Documents, Portsmouth (Cumberland House Museum, Portsmouth, 1956).

The Black Book of Winchester, ed. W. H. B. Bird (Wykeham Press, 1925).

The Parish of Hyde, Winchester, R. F. Penell (Gilbert, 1909).

History of the Andover Grammar School, A. C. Bennett and E. Parsons (Parsons, Andover, 1920).

The Third Book of Remembrance of Southampton 1514–1602, ed. A. L. Merson (Southampton Record Society, 2 vols, 1952, 1955).

XIII

Civil War and Social Change

THE first two Stuart kings of England were often in Hampshire before the outbreak of the Civil War in 1642. In 1603, James I came to Winchester during Sir Walter Raleigh's trial for treason, and his son Charles, Prince of Wales, was given a great welcome at Portsmouth in 1623, for the inhabitants were delighted that he had not succeeded in winning the hand of a Spanish princess. Charles stayed in Southampton, as king, in 1625 and in 1627 and was well received, yet there can be no doubt that his marriage with a Roman Catholic French princess, his religious and financial policies as well as his attempt to rule arbitrarily without a parliament made him very unpopular with many of his Hampshire subjects. When the Civil War broke out in 1642, Hampshire, like many of the English counties, had no hard or fast divisions of classes or districts between King and Parliament. Winchester was famous for its loyalty to the Crown, yet even in that city there were prominent 'Puritans' who disliked the reform of the Church begun by Archbishop Laud, a reform associated in Hampshire with the Dean of Winchester, John Young and Lancelot Andrewes, whom James I made Bishop of Winchester. In Southampton, the Pilgrim Fathers had not been unwelcome when they gathered there to sail from the port in 1620, taking a local youth among the crew; twenty years later that town gave a great welcome to William Prynne the Puritan writer and pamphleteer, on his return from imprisonment in the Channel Islands. There can be little doubt that there were many Hampshire men who felt that they must oppose the King for reasons of religious conscience.

The chief Royalist leader in Hampshire was John Paulet, Marquess of Winchester, whose headquarters were at Basing House, the greatest Royalist strong point in the county.

Other county Royalist families included the Tichbornes, the Sandys of Mottisfont and of The Vyne, the Oglanders of the Isle of Wight, and the commander of the Winchester garrison, Sir William Ogle, but amongst the gentry there were many painful divisions. The Parliamentarian general, Sir William Waller, was a cousin of the loyal Marquess, and brother-in-law to Sir William Ogle. One of the Tichbornes moved far enough away from the family pattern to become a Parliamentarian Lord Mayor of London and to sign Charles I's death warrant. Other county gentlemen who fought against the King included the Flemings of North Stoneham, Colonel Norton of Old Alresford and Southwick Park, and Francis St. Barbe of Broadlands near Romsey.

In both Southampton and Portsmouth there was strong feeling for Parliament. Both had suffered from the burdens of forced loans, from the imposition of ship money, and from the billeting of royal troops. Soon after the outbreak of war both towns capitulated to Parliamentarian demands, and their loss to the King was a vital factor in the eventual defeat of the Royalist forces. Roughly speaking it is perhaps true to suggest that the western half of the county was more Royalist than the east. Support for Parliament was strong in the Isle of Wight and particularly associated with John Lisle of Wootton and his family, though a number of local gentlemen headed by John Oglander, Lisle's godfather, were known to be Royalists.

The surrender of Portsmouth and Southampton, a temporary taking of Winchester and the slighting of Farnham Castle, home of the diocesan bishop, were all early indications of the way in which the war was eventually to go. In 1644 the Royalists suffered a further great defeat at Cheriton. Cheriton was followed by the appearance of Oliver Cromwell on the Hampshire scene, by the surrender of Winchester to him in 1645, and by the fall of Basing House and its almost complete demolition. There was no more real fighting in the county. The King eventually became a prisoner in the Isle of Wight at Carisbrooke Castle, whence he was eventually moved to Hurst Castle. On his journey through the county, to his trial at London, Charles was received with courage and with loyalty by the Winchester Corporation at the Westgate of the city. At near-by Hursley, the squire of the village, Richard Major, was a personal friend of Oliver Cromwell, and Major's daughter, Dorothy, married the Lord Protector's son, Richard. It thus happened that after the Restoration the younger Cromwell spent part of his later years in this Hampshire village, in quiet retirement.

The Restoration of the monarchy in 1660 was undoubtedly a popular event in Hampshire. Many people had lost all for the King or Parliament's sake, and looked forward, in some cases in vain, to a period of restitution and political stability. Sir John Mill, at whose Southampton house the King had dined in 1627, had a son killed at Oxford and was himself ruined by the war, falsely accused of being a Papist, and had his personal property, including the family plate, stripped from him by looting soldiers. He died before the Restoration, with little indeed to leave to his family. At Fareham the Royalist Riggs family lost their entire estate. Amongst the King's supporters Arthur Capell, of Martyr Worthy, was beheaded in Whitehall in March, 1649. Sir John Oglander of Nunwell was almost ruined, was frequently arrested and imprisoned and his children on the mainland found it often impossible to visit him for the double fear of leaving their homes to be rifled by the army or of meeting with soldiers on their way to Nunwell. Between 1642 and 1645 the countryside suffered greatly from the almost constant marching and counter marching of the armies of the Crown and of Parliament, the billeting of soldiers and the general ravages of war; a contemporary observer in 1644 describes Hampshire as practically ruined with nothing left in it for man or beast. One of the saddest aspects of the war was the divisions which it brought into family life. Sir John Oglander had a Parliamentarian brother and his cousin and godson, John Lisle of Wootton in the Isle of Wight (Member of Parliament for Winchester in 1642) was a Cromwellian. Yet all was not bitterness or loss. The close tie of kinship which bound so many of the Hampshire families had a softening influence. Even such an important Hampshire change as the sale of the Sandys' great house of The Vyne to Challoner Chute in 1653 had its mitigating factors, for Chute was acknowledged as the most eminent lawyer in England, and though later to be well known as Speaker of Richard Cromwell's House of Commons he was gratefully remembered in Royalist circles as the advocate who had dared in 1641 to defend 'the Bishops of England in their extreme peril' as well as Archbishop Laud two years later.

Royalist military failure, the legislation of the Long and Rump Parliaments and the death of the King brought therefore many changes to Hampshire. The Bishop of Winchester's castles at Wolvesey and at near-by Farnham in Surrey were 'slighted'; Winchester Castle was virtually demolished and Sir William Waller, who claimed it in his own right, eventually sold the great hall to a group of trustees for the county. The Dean and Chapter of Winchester were abolished, the cathedral left to the preaching and services of ministers, of whom one, Theophilus Gale, a brilliant scholar, eventually founded that Dissenting academy at Stoke Newington which later on had as one of its pupils the most famous of Free Church hymn-writers, Isaac Watts of Southampton. Throughout the county, the Dean and Chapter's many estates were let out to new tenants, the cathedral became dilapidated and was almost demolished in 1653, and the Close was so ruined that much of it had to be pulled down or rebuilt after 1660. The Parliamen-

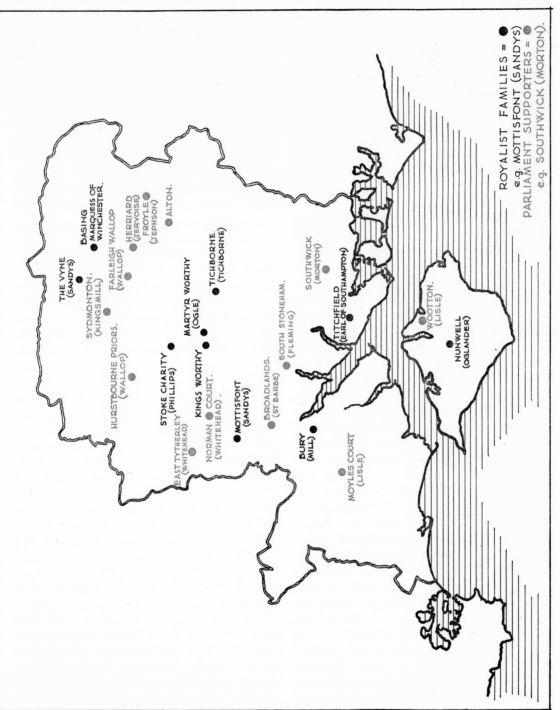

Map 11. Hampshire in the Civil War.

tarian inhabitants of the Close in 1649 included two 'ministers' and John Lisle, the city's Recorder.

A brief word only need be said of Hampshire in the later years of the seventeenth century. Both Winchester and Southampton were involved in the constitutional difficulties with Charles II and James II, and both towns lost their charters.

An extravagant scheme begun by Charles II for making Winchester again the royal capital with a great Versailles type of palace designed by Sir Christopher Wren, and actually begun in 1683, was virtually abandoned in the reign of George I, and the building, left uncompleted, became the nucleus of Winchester Barracks.

Though Hampshire was not concerned in the Monmouth rebellion, John Lisle's widow, Dame Alice Lisle of Moyle's Court, in the New Forest, was accused of harbouring rebels at her home after the defeat at Sedgemoor. She was tried by Judge Jeffries, and executed in the Square in Winchester in 1685. At this notorious trial attempts were made to pack the jury, and to terrify the townspeople by billeting soldiers on them. It was a Winchester member of a very famous Hampshire family, Thomas Wavell, who encouraged his fellow citizens to resist James II's attempts at arbitrary government, though local liberty might have suffered a permanent setback had not the King been forced to flee the country in 1688.

One of the most important results of these failures of royal attempts at arbitrary government was eventually the growth of a strong local government based on democratic local responsibility. Much of this local government, in town and country alike, was carried out by

Justices of the Peace. Justices supervised the records of the parish 'overseers of the poor' who had to collect local poor rates and apprentice poor children: they saw, too, that each local parish surveyor kept his roads in fair repair. Meeting at Quarter Sessions, County Justices supervised the repairs of the County Hall within Winchester Castle, provided accommodation for judges and juries, administered the county jail, suppressed poaching, and administered the few national taxes, for example the Land Tax and the better known Window Tax of William and Mary's reign, which is always blamed for many blocked windows in large houses.

In 1662 a large number of laymen and over two thousand beneficed clergymen in England, unable to accept the liturgy of the new Prayer Book of that year, left the Anglican Church. It is significant that it was the justices, all members of the Established Church, who were given the task of licensing the 'Dissentors' chapels which soon sprang up all over the county. By the end of the seventeenth century, Quarter Sessions Records show that there was little persecution in Hampshire of either Dissentors or Roman Catholics. An era of difficulties and of political and religious conflict gave way, by the beginning of Queen Anne's reign, to a period of tolerance and political quiet.

Further reading: The Civil War in Hampshire, G. N. Godwin (Gilbert, Southampton, 1904).
Southampton Essays: 'Southampton in the Seventeenth Century', L. Burgess (1958).
History of Fareham, G. Privett (Wykeham Press, 1949).
Dean Young's Diary, ed. F. Goodman (S.P.C.K., 1923).
Quarter Sessions Government in Hampshire in the Seventeenth Century, ed. J. S. Furley (Warren & Son).

XIV

Writers of History and Makers of Maps 1575–1869

FROM the days when the anonymous compilers of the *Anglo-Saxon Chronicle* were writing down their great record, Hampshire has never lacked historians. In the twelfth and thirteenth centuries the professional writers of history were monks, keeping monastic chronicles which described the most important local and national events of their times. One of the most famous of these chroniclers was Richard of Devizes, a monk of the Cathedral Priory at Winchester, who not only wrote a famous account of Richard I and his Crusades, but was also responsible for a great many pages in the year by year record kept in the cathedral. These *Annales Wintonie*, the Winchester Annals, are a basis for much local history and in particular record the architectural history of the cathedral. Towards the end of the medieval period another Winchester monk, Thomas Rudbourne, writing in the first half of the fifteenth century and having before him earlier documents which have since been lost, wrote an account of the history of the cathedral and its traditions, and challenged the accounts of British history given by Geoffrey of Monmouth and in particular that writer's fantastic accounting of the fabled King Arthur.

In the sixteenth and early seventeenth centuries it was not always wise to write about contemporary politics or recent history. It was safer to write the early history of Britain as did Richard White of Basingstoke (1539–1611), a wealthy Hampshire gentleman who spent most of his life in exile because he was a Roman Catholic; White's history of England before the Norman Conquest contains much about King Arthur, whose Round Table, on the west wall of Winchester Castle did a good deal to encourage Hampshire's interest in early British heroes. The Tudor kings were anxious to establish themselves as a family of ancient lineage and

Henry VIII's elder brother, who died before their father, was actually christened Arthur in Winchester Cathedral. In 1522 Henry proudly showed the table to his guest, the Emperor Charles V, whose own family, the Hapsburgs, unlike the Tudors, were of known and anciently established descent.

About one hundred and fifty years later, a Winchester lawyer, John Trussell (died *c.* 1648) also made use of some of the earlier British legends of local and national history. Trussell's continuation of Daniel's *Collections* of English History was made recommended reading by at least one tutor in the University of Cambridge, and his brief Catalogue of Winchester City Muniments contained in a manuscript which now belongs to an American, is one of the earliest lists of its kind in the county. Like Richard White, Trussell came from a Roman Catholic family but he himself conformed to the Anglican Church, becoming Clerk to the Dean and Chapter of Winchester Cathedral, and Mayor of the city in 1624–5 and 1633–4.

A later Clerk to the Dean and Chapter, John Chase, who died in 1658, made an even more valuable contribution to Hampshire history, for he compiled a complete catalogue of the cathedral's archives; his *List of Muniments* is thus a wonderful source book for Hampshire's history since the documents he describes were ransacked and partially destroyed by Cromwellian soldiers in 1642 and 1645. Chase was turned out of the Close, but his interest in local history continued. He became churchwarden of St. John in the Soke, and compiled a very useful list of all the documents belonging to his parish church, an example of what could have been done in other Hampshire parishes had other churchwardens followed his example. Trussell and Chase were both consciously thinking of the historian's duty to the future as was another and more famous Royalist, John Oglander (1585–1655) of Nunwell in the Isle of Wight, when he compiled his 'Rules for a Happy Life' for his three-year-old son. Oglander had indeed a deep and conscious sense of the continuity and devotion to public duty needed in a great private family, and his papers are a vital source for the years of the Civil War in Hampshire and the Isle of Wight, as is the diary of yet another contemporary Royalist, John Young, Dean of Winchester Cathedral, who was turned out by the Parliamentarians and who died before the Restoration. The Civil War and the Restoration, by their very controversial nature, aroused great interest in national and in Hampshire history. One of the most famous works of the time was *The History of the Rebellion* by the Earl of Clarendon, and Clarendon was also interested in Hampshire, where he owned property and where his cousin Alexander Hyde was Dean of Winchester from 1660 till 1665. He began to write a history of the cathedral, but it was not finished when he died and had to be completed by Samuel Gale in 1715. This is the first real printed history of the cathedral, and it has many interesting illustrations.

From this time onwards there continued to be many professional men, lawyers, doctors, or ecclesiastics, to whom the study or writing of local history was an important hobby. In 1759 Doctor John Speed, a physician practising in Southampton where he was an honorary burgess, wrote a learned account of Charles I's charter to the town, and in about 1770 completed a small folio history of Southampton illustrated by three maps and containing an index. Speed's *History* has proved its worth as the basis of much later works on Southampton and was indeed much used in that town's standard *History* compiled by the Rev. J. S. Davies in 1883. One of the most famous town histories of the eighteenth century was Bishop John Milner's account of Winchester; Milner, the Catholic priest in charge of the Roman community in Winchester put his great work together in less than twelve months, with the result that the first edition 1798 has many inaccuracies, and even the later editions suffered from the fact that Milner made much use of Trussell's Winchester manuscript, for Trussell, for all his very good qualities, could often neither interpret nor translate the medieval documents he had before him.

A more professional historian, with wider Hampshire interests, was Richard Warner of Sway in the New Forest. Warner was interested in and wrote about the Forest, the Isle of Wight, the site of Clausentum, the history of Netley Abbey, and the Hampshire section of Domesday Book, which he published in 1789 with an English translation. In 1792, a much smaller printed work on *Clausentum* contained with it Warner's proposals for a general history of Hampshire, and this proposal was put into effect in 1795 by the publication in six volumes of *Collections for the History of Hampshire and the Bishopric of Winchester*. Warner in fact described this work as 'a bare faced piracy' published without his comment or knowledge, but whatever its actual origin, it was undoubtedly inspired by him and was a most important step forward in the writing of Hampshire history. In 1840 Robert Mudie brought out his *Hampshire*, a topographical history in three volumes including the Isle of Wight, and charmingly illustrated by a series of fine and illuminating drawings. The whole technique and standard of historical writing received a tremendous stimulus in the 1850s, when the Rev. D. D. Woodward (1816–1869), with T. C. Wilks and C. Lockart, published a magnificent but undated three volume *History of Hampshire*. Anyone who wishes to know what Victorian Hampshire looked like must consult these early and important histories. Woodward was Librarian to Queen Victoria at Windsor Castle and his work on Hampshire did much to prepare the way for the five great volumes of the County History named in honour of the Queen, and published as the *Victoria County History of Hampshire* between 1900 and 1914.

Parallel with this growth in the writing of

history came another development of local knowledge, the consideration of the geographical features of Hampshire, and the careful compilation of general maps and road books for travellers and of detailed surveys of estates belonging to private landowners.

Christopher Saxton's map of Hampshire drawn in 1575 for his great *Atlas* of County Maps published in 1579 does not show roads, but it does include bridges which must indicate the existence of roads. Early road books, dating from 1541, give the distances between stages on the main roads and it is interesting that until 1675 no road book shows a road going through the county capital. On the two main routes through the county, London-Exeter, London-Southampton, Winchester was apparently by-passed in the best modern manner, travellers from London to the West going via Basingstoke and Andover, whilst from London to Southampton the route went through Alresford and Twyford. In 1675 John Ogilvy's *Britannia* showed three routes through Winchester and five other main roads in the county. Hampshire roads are first clearly marked on a map drawn by Robert Morden for Camden's *Brittania* (1695). By 1742, when Herman Moll published a Hampshire map in his *Atlas* (*A description of England and Wales*), there were seventeen main routes in the county of which ten passed through Winchester. Moll's map is interesting too, in that it was adorned with a number of objects of antiquity, indicative of the interests of the county gentlemen who bought the *Atlas*. Isaac Taylor's large and beautiful map of

Hampshire, drawn in 1759, has a further interest since it marks the country houses of the landed gentry. Maps like these, and road books, were of great importance, for improvements in transport were already helping to make possible the important changes in agriculture which helped to bring about the agrarian revolution.

At the same time as these great maps were being drawn, surveys of private estates made by professional surveyors for corporate bodies or private owners provide a wealth of detailed information about certain areas. Particular mention ought to be made of the work of William Godson, in the middle of the eighteenth century. He carried out a complete survey of the many Hampshire estates of the Dean and Chapter, drew a careful map of the City of Winchester for the Corporation there, and his other commissions included surveys of estates at Houghton and at Chawton, later to be Jane Austen's village. Surveys like these with their details of footpaths, varied uses of land, woods, and common land, are a particularly useful source for any study of Hampshire agricultural history, as are the maps which accompany enclosure awards and the later series showing how Hampshire tithes were apportioned.

Further reading: Dean Young's Diary, ed. F. Goodman (S.P.C.K., 1927).
'Hampshire in early maps and early road books', E. G. Box (H.F.C. *Proceedings*, Vol. XII, pt. 3, 1934).
Speed's History of Southampton, ed. E. R. Aubrey (Southampton Record Society, 1909).

XV

Change in the Eighteenth Century: Transport and Agriculture

IF most of the seventeenth century can be described as an age of conflict, the century that followed was a period of revolution, revolution in politics and revolutionary change in methods of transport, of agriculture, and of industry.

Some account has already been given of the surveyors and map makers of eighteenth-century Hampshire. In one way their work was part of the great revolution in methods of transport which began in the eighteenth century and which is still going on today. Change came first in alterations to roads and to bridges, and by the provision of canals, though Hampshire was never a real canal county. Amongst the rebuilt bridges can be noticed that over the river Meon at Wickham (1762 with later additions) and various bridges over the Itchen rebuilt in the nineteenth century including the Soke Bridge at Winchester designed by George Forder in 1813, and very largely financed by public subscription. Many of the bridges over the Test were built or rebuilt in the late eighteenth century, Stockbridge in 1799, Redbridge, which had been destroyed in the Civil War, was a single span in 1793; and Middle Bridge over the Test at Romsey was designed by the County Surveyor, Milne, in 1783. The bridge at Lymington, an important link in Hampshire coastal connections, was constructed much later, in 1860, and took the place of a ferry. The county, under the county justices and through its County Treasurer, spent money regularly on the upkeep of certain main bridges, the chief being those at Redbridge, Fordingbridge, Christchurch, Ringwood and Stockbridge.

In country districts improvements to main roads were usually financed by money collected at tollgates and turnpikes set up by a long series of Acts of Parliament. Quarter Sessions records show the difficulties of repairs, but improvements in surfacing and drainage by the construction of roads with cambers slowly continued. In towns, Paving Commissioners, ancestors of modern Highways Committees, were empowered to improve roads and to license sedan chairs and hackney carriages and the commissioners also controlled alterations to all house frontages, including the making of bow windows. As roads improved facilities for travellers improved likewise, and many Hampshire coaching inns, amongst them the Black Swan at Winchester, the Dolphin at Southampton, the George at Portsmouth, became nationally famous. Towns were linked by regular services and *A Guide to Coaches* published in 1753 gives a long list of towns in alphabetical order with the names of the inns in London from which their coach services started. Small parcels and perishable goods and even the poorer traveller went by carrier. Amongst the most successful eighteenth-century carriers were the Waldrons of Winchester, whose firm carried goods for the Dean and Chapter from the Restoration onwards. Three members of the family were mayors of Winchester, and after the death of Thomas Waldron in 1775 the business was continued by other families from the same premises.

Heavy non-perishable commodities could be more easily moved by water. In 1767 an Act for Making Divers Rivers Navigable applied to the Itchen, though there had been attempts to canalize that river as early as the reign of Charles I. The Basingstoke Canal was more successful than the scheme for a canal linking Portsmouth to London, but it soon became apparent that the terrain of Hampshire was not really suitable for canals, and in the nineteenth century Hampshire canals soon gave way to railways.

One result of the improvements in road conditions was that a great number of ob-

20. Alice Lisle. 21. L. D. G. Tregonwell.

19. Dorothy Cromwell. 22. Charlotte M. Yonge.

Dorothy Cromwell (née Major, died 1676) of Hursley, wife of the second Lord Protector, Richard Cromwell. Alice Lisle of Moyle's Court, Ringwood, executed Winchester 1685. L. D. G. Tregonwell, Esq., 1758–1832, 'Founder' of Bournemouth. Charlotte M. Yonge, 1823–1901, from the portrait by George Richmond.

23. The High Street, Southampton, in *c.* 1840.

24. The Cathedral at Portsmouth, incorporating the ancient parish church of St. Thomas of Canterbury.

25. The Docks at Southampton, October 1962, showing the 83,000-ton Cunarder *Queen Elizabeth* about to leave for New York.

servers travelled through Hampshire leaving behind some delightful contemporary accounts of what they saw. Celia Fiennes indeed visited the county at the end of the seventeenth century without much comfort, riding everywhere on the horse immortalized in the Banbury Cross nursery rhyme. Born in 1662 near Salisbury, Celia came from a well-known Parliamentarian family, her mother being Frances Whitehead of West Tytherley in Hampshire. Most of her 'Journal' in which she describes her many journeys was written in 1702; written in a vigorous style its Hampshire sections depict such various subjects as the great house at Broadlands belonging to her St. Barbe relations, the salt industry of Lymington, the decline of Southampton, and naval scenes at Portsmouth. Daniel Defoe (1661–1731) cast a townsman's eye on Hampshire, where waste of land in the New Forest horrified him and

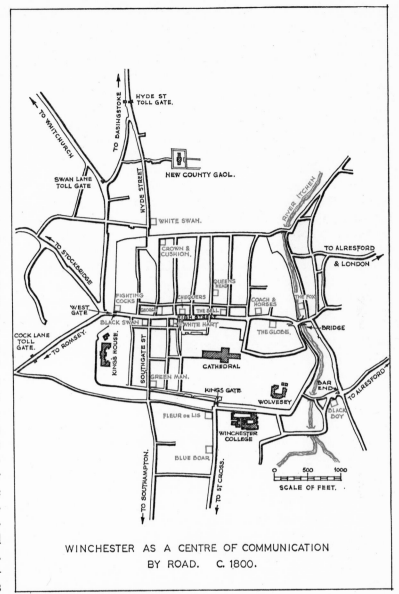

WINCHESTER AS A CENTRE OF COMMUNICATION BY ROAD. C. 1800.

Map 12. Winchester as a Coaching Centre. (Compare the grid plan with that of Silchester, p. 13.)

he suggested a scheme for redeveloping it as small holdings, which fortunately remained only on paper. He noticed, too, the manufacture of cloth at Basingstoke and the disastrous fire (one of a series) which had ravaged Alresford. Changes in agriculture were of interest to many travellers and writers, and amongst the most famous of these observers

was Arthur Young, whose *Six Weeks Tour* of 1767 gives some detailed accounts of improvements in agriculture, the introduction of new crops, the fair state of certain Hampshire roads, and the current prices of farm produce and of agricultural wages. In the Romsey district the ordinary labourer could hope for about seven shillings a week, and in the

E

countryside around Winchester and Romsey most of the farms were small. Another observer, later in the century, William Marshall, described the hop gardens of northern Hampshire in the areas around Bentley, Froyle and Alton where large quantities of hops were sold each year at Weyhill Fair, near Andover. At a still later date Hampshire agriculture was described in detail by Charles Vancouver in his *A General View of Agriculture of the County of Hampshire*. Vancouver's book was published in 1813, and by the beginning of the nineteenth century some of the general effects of the changes leading up to the agrarian revolution were beginning to be felt in Hampshire, though the county was perhaps never subject to the degree of change to be found in other parts of England.

An important part of agrarian change was the enclosure movement. These enclosures of common land were for improvement, not just for sheep farming, as they had been in the Tudor period, and were carried out either by Act of Parliament, or by mutual consent, or in some cases illegally. To enclose land was very expensive for the small yeoman farmer, and small farms were swallowed up by larger landlords. Side by side with enclosures went improvements in farming methods. Crops and stock changed, and machinery was introduced into a way of life which had relied almost entirely on the labour of men's hands. One of the earliest Hampshire farmers to vary and improve his crops was Edward Lisle of Crux Easton in the north of the county. Lisle, a descendant of the famous Hampshire family, grew turnips and a variety of new grains, clover, rye grass and sainfoin for example, and also used malt dust as a fertilizer. In south Hampshire Crown lands were in especially poor condition and in need of improvements and in the New Forest in particular there were too many deer and not enough really good timber for the Royal Navy. Yet the south was apparently enclosed earlier than the rest of the county, and the effect of enclosure was almost always better production. Even in Vancouver's

time, however, a large area round Portsmouth still preserved the open-three-field system, though much of the fallow was used successfully for market gardening to produce supplies for the rapidly increasing population of Portsmouth. Root crops were being grown everywhere, turnips, swedes and kohl-rabi and regional crops included not only hops near Farnham but also cabbages grown for the patients of the Royal Naval Hospital at Haslar and the Royal County Hospital at Winchester.

Agricultural implements were changing rapidly, but new farming equipment and machinery was expensive and only a wealthy landowner could afford to have the threshing mills Vancouver noticed at Abbotstone, Twyford and Tichborne. Though it was becoming usual to roll the land with rollers of wood and iron, the varieties of Hampshire soil made different types of plough essential, and there were many varieties of light plough, as well as a heavy plough, two wheeled and drawn by four horses.

Hampshire has no indigenous breed of cattle. Many farmers in the eighteenth and early nineteenth centuries used their animals for draught and then 'finished' them for beef; special milking herds were only slowly introduced. Vancouver found herds of Guernseys at farms at Lymington and Milford and in the same year that his book was published an Ovington farmer offered a few Alderney cows for sale, by advertisement in the *Hampshire Chronicle*. Vancouver thought poorly of Hampshire horses, though pigs were being improved in his time by cross-breeding, and a diet of apples which was said to give a better taste to the bacon. As far as sheep were concerned, the county was roughly divided into two sections at the villages of East and West Meon. The small heath sheep of the west slowly disappeared, as the Southdown flocks from the east spread along the chalk hills and became famous flocks if, indeed, they belonged to prominent owners like Sir Thomas Miller or Sir Henry Tichborne.

All these many changes brought their own

social problems in a county where agriculture was the staple industry. For most of the period, too, England was at war with France, and high prices, low wages, unemployment, the disappearance of the small independent yeoman farmer, brought about a migration from countryside to town and from the south to the north of England where employment in new industries was more certain though not less strenuous. Increasing burdens fell on to the already creaking machinery of local government and on to the overburdened shoulders of the Justices of the Peace. Immediately after the end of the war with France in 1815 there were many farming bankruptcies, followed by riots against the introduction of machinery, and the imprisonment of farm labourers involved in these demonstrations. It soon became clear that new kinds of social-political problems would have to be faced and solved. No one was more conscious of the difficulties of the times in so far as they concerned the ordinary working man than William Cobbett, of whose Hampshire connections something will be said in a later chapter. Cobbett died in 1835, but he lived long enough to see his most disliked crop, the potato, strongly established in Hampshire; it became part of the agricultural worker's staple diet, and was grown on a large scale around Whitchurch from about 1836 onwards.

By the middle of the nineteenth century farming in the Isle of Wight was said to be about a hundred years behind the times, but even on the mainland, within the county proper, there were still many local variations, and few farmers were able to manage their estates as effectively as the Duke of Wellington who rebuilt farm-houses and labourers' cottages, and drained and chalked his tenants' farms at his own expense. Generally speaking, however, in mid-Victorian Hampshire, the farmers in the south were more prosperous than those in the north, wages were higher, housing conditions better, though one feature of southern farming, the typical water meadows of the river valleys which had produced good lambs for the London market and valuable early hay crops, began to decline when the coming of the railways altered the market. The railways, too, helped to bring a slow end to the old Hampshire fairs which had once played such a distinctive role in the county's agriculture.

Further reading: *The Journeys of Celia Fiennes*, ed. C. Morris (Cresset Press, 1947).
'Four Centuries of Farming Systems in Hampshire, 1500–1900', G. E. Fussell (H.F.C. *Proceedings*, XVIII, Pt. 3, 1952).
A General View of the Agriculture of Hampshire and the Isle of Wight, Charles Vancouver (1813).

XVI

The Industrial Revolution and the Growth of Towns

THE Hampshire countryside was comparatively unaltered in appearance by the early years of the Industrial Revolution to which the long series of wars with France formed part of the political background. One of Hampshire's most successful industries was in fact greatly increased in importance by a refugee Frenchman, Henri de Portal, a Huguenot, who came to Southampton with his brother to escape persecution. Henri obtained work as an apprentice at a paper mill at South Stoneham and in 1712 opened his own paper-making mill at Bere Mill on the Test near Whitchurch. He thus laid the foundations of the success of a famous family and a famous industry which today makes banknote paper for many different countries as well as for the Bank of England. For this particular industry a good water supply is an absolute necessity, and from the middle of the seventeenth century onwards the many streams of Hampshire supplied a variety of paper mills.

Another long-established Hampshire industry was shipbuilding, and war with France brought prosperity to many a small Hampshire shipyard. Private yards flourished, for they were able to build ships of moderate size and were in easy reach of the timber of the New Forest. At Buckler's Hard near Beaulieu in the New Forest, the Adams family built ships for the Royal Navy including the *Illustrious*, wrecked in 1795, and *Agamemnon*, the first ship of the line to be commanded by Nelson. At Bursledon, the firm of Parsons built the *Elephant*, Nelson's flagship at Copenhagen, and many other famous ships. These firms were small family businesses, but at Portsmouth the Lords of the Admiralty had to expand the Dockyard and began to employ labour, skilled and unskilled on a large scale. Soon Portsea Island was no longer large enough for the increasing

needs of the population, and much of the adjacent mainland had to be devoted to the growing of market garden produce to feed the rapidly increasing population, a population which included former agricultural labourers who could only find employment in large towns. In 1848 Queen Victoria opened the Steam Basin at Portsmouth and a short time afterwards dry docks were included amongst the many Dockyard extensions and alterations. The Royal Navy Gunnery School started in 1832 on H.M.S. *Excellent* was transferred to Whale Island, which was re-inforced with soil dug out of the docks by convict labour from the grim prison hulks near-by. Though in 1811 the population of Portsea Island was a mere 34,484, by 1851 it had almost doubled, and in 1901 was 180,800. Incidentally the figures for 1811 include an estimate for over a thousand convicts living in hulks, for one of the major social difficulties of the early nineteenth century was the provision of proper prison accommodation. Bridewells at Gosport, Odiham and Winchester were inadequate, and a new county gaol was erected in Winchester in 1857.

Portsmouth grew because of war, Southampton very largely because of the revolution in transport which soon made that town one of the chief commercial ports in the kingdom, though by the second half of the eighteenth century it seemed as if Southampton's revival would be as a fashionable watering place, for sea bathing from the western shore was tried out by the Prince of Wales in 1750, and he returned many times. Sea baths were built, and invalids came in crowds to benefit by them, as did in other ways many well-known local doctors including John Speed, the historian of Southampton; Jane Austen was another famous visitor. Assemblies, balls, and all kinds of social activities were encouraged by

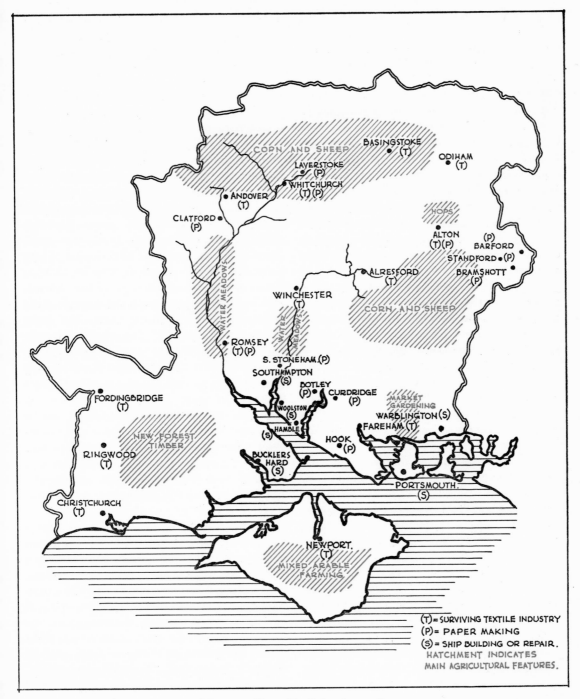

Map 13. Hampshire Industries, c 1815.

occasional visits from Royalty and by the interesting if eccentric second Marquess of
Lansdowne, who built himself a mock Gothic

castle on the older fortification on Castle
Hill. But the future of Southampton did not
depend on the patronage of its visitors,

commerce and overseas trade were more important and other south coast watering places soon became more fashionable. In 1820 the town was lit by gas from a gasometer only eighty-four feet high, and a chain pier was opened in 1833 by the Duchess of Kent, Victoria's mother, both improvements which attracted visitors, but which also preceded the rapid development of the port. A dock company was incorporated in 1836, the first stone of the New Dock laid in 1838, a Tidal Dock begun in 1839, the first dry dock opened in 1846. The completion of the London-Southampton railway line assured Southampton's future as a great commercial port and as well as docks and railways, other nineteenth-century additions to Southampton still continue to add to the town's prosperity. The Ordnance Survey Office was established in 1841 by four companies of the Royal Engineers and on 15th October, 1862, Lord Palmerston opened the Hartley Institute in the High Street, named after its benefactor, Henry Hartley, a successful business man who had left money to the Corporation for the development of learning. This Hartley Institute was to form the nucleus of the University of Southampton.

Smaller Hampshire towns were also affected by the coming of the railway and grew in size and importance. Belief in the virtues of sea air and of sea bathing, a fashion which had already affected the growth of Southampton, led also to developments on other parts of the Hampshire coast. George III visited Mudeford in 1803 and it was from this fashionable village that Mr. L. D. G. Tregonwell (1758–1852) drove to 'Bourne' in 1810, decided to build himself a house there, and so laid the foundation of the future prosperity of Bournemouth. The name Bournemouth appears to go back to at least 1574, when the area was known for its copperas works at Boscombe and Brownsea Island; two hundred years later the staple industry was smuggling, a highly organized and profitable occupation for such well-known characters as Old Gulliver and Slippery Rogers.

The erection of a family mansion at Bourne Tregonwell, a name soon discarded in favour of 'Bournemouth', assured the village of a wholly respectable future. Tregonwell was the wealthy head of a well-known Dorset family, and he set a fashion soon followed by others. His house was completed in 1812, and soon after the Lord of the Manor of Westover, Sir George Ivison Tapps, who owned the whole of the sea front, laid out much of the area to the design of an eminent architect from Christchurch, Mr. B. Ferrey. The Bath Hotel, built in 1837, was opened on the Coronation Day of Queen Victoria in 1838. Soon the district was famous, not only for its natural advantages of delightful scenery and good climate, but also for its hotels and large detached private houses standing in their own gardens, all set within a landscape carefully and constantly replanted with pine trees. Ferrey's successor was Decimus Burton, who suggested a carriage bridge over the Bourne stream, later developed into what is now The Square. The proper bridging of the Bourne did much to encourage visitors, as did the erection of a jetty, and in 1861 a wooden pier allowed pleasure steamers to land their passengers in safety and comfort. The fashion for seaside holidays and the fact that steamers and railways were available for the use of visitors to Bournemouth were all factors which helped to make certain the future successful development of the town. Eastleigh shows a different aspect of the Industrial Revolution, and grew on land which was part of the ancient manor of Eastleigh and the parish of Bishopstoke, land over which passed the London to Southampton railway, opened in 1840. In the sixteenth century the manor of Eastleigh had passed to the Wells family at Brambridge, and in 1763 to Amy Wells's cousin, Walter Smythe, whose daughter was the famous Mrs. Fitzherbert. By 1864 Thomas Chamberlayne had acquired the manor. He began to grant building leases in the area and the growth of Eastleigh proper was rapid indeed after the London and South Western Railway Company decided in the late 1880's, to move their carriage and wagon works from Nine Elms to Bishopstoke. Much of late Victorian Eastleigh was constructed by builders whose names are recalled by the terraces which they built to house the families of workers employed by the railway. Farther north, railways made possible the establishment of a great military camp at Aldershot in 1854, on vast tracts of undeveloped land purchased by the Government.

Winchester was perhaps of all Hampshire towns the least altered by the Industrial Revolution. One of the few factories to employ children as well as men and women, however, was the silk mill in St. Peter Street, which moved to larger premises in Abbey Mill in 1793. Where industry increased in Winchester it increased on the traditional lines of industries already established and properly to be found in the county's market town. There were no fewer than six printing firms in Winchester in 1859, and one of these, Jacob & Johnson, had taken over the county newspaper, the *Hampshire Chronicle*, in 1813. Breweries and malting houses increased in number, and there was employment for manual labour in the leather trades and in brickmakers' yards.

In general, the Industrial Revolution greatly increased the size of the larger Hampshire towns, encouraged the growth of new towns and also helped to make possible a definite movement of population away from the countryside. Even the smaller towns helped to depopulate the neighbouring villages. A variety of industries, scattered in many parts of the county, reflected the needs of an increasing population. Bricks were urgently needed for the new and not always very attractive artisans' dwellings springing up in Portsmouth, Southampton and Eastleigh. There were famous Victorian brick kilns at Chandler's Ford and at Fareham. Vast quantities of beer and ale were brewed in Ringwood, Romsey, Basingstoke and Havant, as well as in Winchester, and this industry can be deemed a natural one in a county which grows good barley, good hops, and has a good water supply. To a certain limited extent, brewing has taken part of the pre-eminent place formerly held by the cloth industry. By the middle of the nineteenth century few small Hampshire towns had much left in the way of the textile and weaving domestic industries which had once been a chief factor in their prosperity. In the early Victorian period bags for hops were made at Alton, stockings were knitted at Christchurch and at Ringwood, some bed-ticking woven at Fordingbridge, and special kinds of silk made at Overton, Whitchurch and Winchester, but the deservedly famous cloths of medieval Hampshire had long disappeared and the textile industry was firmly established in the north of England.

Further reading: 'Paper Mills in Hampshire', A. H. Shorter (H.F.C. *Proceedings*, XVIII, Pt. 1, 1953).
Canals of Southern England, Charles Hadfield (Phoenix House, 1955).
The English Prison Hulks, W. Branch-Johnson (Johnson, 1957).
The Story of Bournemouth, David S. Young (Robert Hale, 1957).
Bournemouth, 1810–1910, C. H. Mate and C. Riddle (Mate and Sons, 1910).
The South Western Railway, Hamilton Ellis (Allen & Unwin, 1956).
The Story of Aldershot, Howard N. Cole (Gale & Polden, 1951).
The University of Southampton, 1862–1962, A. T. Paterson (University of Southampton, 1962).

XVII

Social Problems and Public Life in Early Victorian Hampshire

BY the end of the first quarter of the nineteenth century the ever-increasing populations of Hampshire towns were creating new and urgent social difficulties. Bad living conditions, particularly in the dock areas of Portsmouth and Southampton, were made worse by lack of education and the inability of unreformed local and national government to deal with these problems. In the countryside standards of living were poor and the important changes which made up the agrarian revolution were viewed with suspicion by the labouring classes. There were widespread agricultural riots, notorious riots at Barton Stacey, Holybourne, Hawkley and Selborne, and in 1830, fourteen agricultural labourers were actually sentenced to death for their part in the rebellions. The feelings of the time are reflected in the serious and moral attitude of the local press which often had to report ghastly crimes, yet was never sensational or lurid. Local newspapers with long histories, and still in existence, include the *Salisbury and Winchester Journal*, established in Salisbury in 1729, the *Hampshire Telegraph* (Portsmouth, 1799) and the county newspaper, the *Hampshire Chronicle* printed at Southampton in 1772, but since 1778 published from Winchester. A successful, independent and impartial local press has thus always played its part in the development of Hampshire's social conscience. The House of Commons and local government in boroughs were reformed in 1832 and 1835. Yet this political reform, important as it was, could never have been successful had it not been accompanied by the development of public conscience, by the growth of enlightened public opinion, by the revival of the Established Church, and by the traditions of public service established and maintained by some notable Hampshire familes.

There can be no doubt that one of the most important critics of the Hampshire scene at the beginning of the nineteenth century was William Cobbett (1763–1835), journalist, politician, and unsuccessful farmer, the self-taught son of a farm labourer. Like Defoe, Cobbett rode all over Hampshire, but unlike that earlier writer, he was a countryman born and bred, and his *Rural Rides* are essential reading for anyone interested in this period of Hampshire history. He was a politician, as well as a journalist, and defender of what he considered to be fundamental rights of every Englishman, and his great contribution to history was his championship of the English yeoman. He disliked 'paper money' and the Hampshire family who manufactured it—'Squire Portal of Rag Castle'; he suspected absentee landlords, amongst them the Ogles of Worthy Park. By the accession of Victoria, much of the property in Hampshire formerly held by Paulets had passed to various members of the great banking family of Baring. Francis Baring, the first baronet (1740–1810) was said to be worth over £7 million. His elder grandson, also Francis (1796–1866) was a Wykehamist, M.P. for Portsmouth from 1826 to 1865, and became first Lord Northbrook, dying at Stratton Park, which had been designed for him by the architect George Dance the younger. Lord Northbrook's uncle, Alexander Baring, the first Lord Ashburton, married Anne Bingham, of Philadelphia, built up a fine library, was a patron of the arts, and a Trustee of the British Museum, and of the National Gallery. His son, William Bingham Baring (1799–1864) lived at the Grange, near Alresford, which he had made a centre for famous literary men, including Buller, Thackeray and Carlyle. Cobbett recognized the kindness and generosity of the Barings and their tenants, but he was suspicious of them as

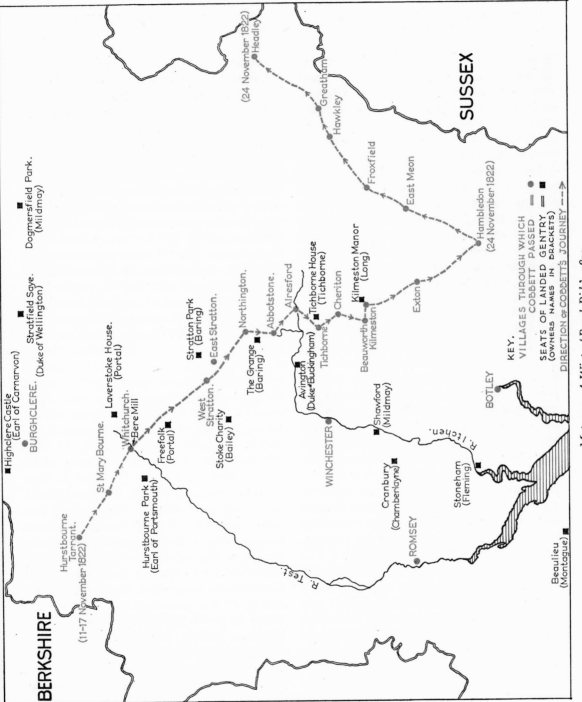

BERKSHIRE

SUSSEX

■ Highclere Castle
(Earl of Carnarvon)

● BURGHCLERE.

● Stratfield Saye.
(Duke of Wellington)

■ Dogmersfield Park.
(Mildmay)

Hurstbourne
Tarrant.
(11-17 November 1822)

St Mary Bourne.

■ Laverstoke House.
(Portal)

Whitchurch.
■ Bere Mill

■ Hurstbourne Park
(Earl of Portsmouth)

■ Freefolk
(Portal)

West
Stratton.

● Stoke Charity
(Bailey)

● East Stratton.

■ Stratton Park
(Baring)

● Northington.

The Grange
(Baring)

● Abbotstone.

Alresford

Avington
(Duke of Buckingham)

Tichborne
(Tichborne)

■ Tichborne House.
(Tichborne)

● Cheriton

● Kilmeston Manor.
(Long)

Beauworth
Kilmeston

● Exton

Hambledon
(24 November 1822)

● East Meon

Froxfield

Hawkley

Greatham

Headley
(24 November 1822)

WINCHESTER

Shawford
(Mildmay)

R. Itchen.

Cranbury
(Chamberlayne)

Stoneham
(Fleming)

BOTLEY

ROMSEY

R. Test.

Beaulieu
(Montague)

KEY.
VILLAGES THROUGH WHICH
COBBETT PASSED

SEATS OF LANDED GENTRY
(OWNERS NAMES IN BRACKETS)

DIRECTION OF COBBETT'S JOURNEY ---->

Map 14. A Winter 'Rural Ride', 1822.

bankers, users of cheques and paper money, and also because he felt they might apply political pressure as an accompaniment of social relief. He had heard good of 'Sir Somebody Tichborne' (in fact, Sir Henry, the 8th Baronet) whose vast estates ran near the Baring land, but observed their broken fences with regret as a sign of this ancient family's impoverishment. In fact the Tichbornes were not poor, but a little later on the estate was much harmed by the famous and long-drawn-out case of the Tichborne claimant who declared himself to be the rightful heir to the baronetcy. Cobbett was prepared to offer advice to anybody about anything, but as a farmer at Botley he was himself a failure, and not all his criticisms were fair; he disliked the first Duke of Wellington, who was an admirable landlord.

The name of Sir William Heathcote (1801–81) of Hursley Park still remains as the very prototype of a Victorian squire in Hampshire and his obituary in *The Times* refers to him as the perfect pattern of an English country gentleman. After he succeeded to the family baronetcy in 1825 he built up a large estate suitable for a landlord who was also a Member of Parliament and a Justice of the Peace, erecting for his tenants the picturesque cottages and lodges which are still such an attractive part of the Hursley neighbourhood. Yet for all his generosity and kindness, he would not tolerate a Nonconformist workman on his estate, and all his employees had to be practising members of the Church of England. Farther east, near Petersfield and at Buriton another great mid-Victorian estate of over six thousand acres was created by the Bonham-Carter family. John Bonham-Carter was Member of Parliament for Winchester between 1847 and 1874 and built himself a large Victorian mansion at Adhurst St. Mary, near Petersfield. This family had a strong link with Portsmouth, where reforming Carters had filled the Corporation with their nominees, but they eventually established their own liberal and politically Liberal traditions

in local government based on principles of democratic government derived from their experiences as Dissenters or rather as Unitarians.

In other Hampshire towns too, there were families prepared to implement the Reform Act of 1832, and to see that the Municipal Corporation Act of 1835 really did have an effect on local government, but open voting, intimidation and even bribery and corruption of electors remained too frequently a picture of local government for many years after the Acts. In the later eighteenth century Winchester affairs had been much influenced by the Chandos family of near-by Avington House, and the daughter of the last Duke of Chandos, Ann, wife of the first Duke of Buckingham and Chandos was much loved in Winchester where one of her interests was the City Police, one of the earliest forces to be set up in the country. Her husband was a Tory, who found his party opposed in Winchester by intellectual Whigs including Charles Shaw Le Fevre, M.P. for the county in 1832 and Samuel Deverall, a Winchester lawyer. When Avington was sold in 1848 the Buckingham-Chandos influence gave way to that of the liberal John Bonham-Carter.

There was thus never a time when 'eighteenth-century jobbery and snobbery' were the only contributions of the Hampshire gentry to local society, and the first County Hospital to be established outside of London was set up in Winchester in 1736 under the continuous patronage of Church and gentry. Moreover, the Established Church was never wholly indifferent to the needs of its people. Gilbert White of Selborne (1720–93) was a good clergyman as well as a great naturalist, and even as an absentee clergyman like the Reverend Philip Williams, Rector of Compton from 1781 to 1830, took great care to arrange for the work of his parish. In early Victorian Hampshire the Reverend John Keble, Vicar of Hursley and a prominent leader of the High Church revival and a writer of many famous hymns, was greatly admired and respected, though a figure of suspicion to some low churchmen. One of Keble's family friends was Charlotte Yonge of Otterbourne House, herself a well-known authoress, and a close friend also of the Heathcotes at Hursley and of the Headmaster of Winchester, George Moberley and his large family. In other parts of the county there were distinguished Anglican clergy who, like Keble, were national figures, but who were 'low church', that is Evangelical leaders, who followed the teachings of Charles Simeon. In Winchester, Simeon's biographer Canon Carus, built a new church and created a new parish, that of Christ Church. At Eversley, in the north of the county, Charles Kingsley, author of *The Water Babies* and other famous books, was a beloved figure, curate and afterwards rector from 1844 to 1875, as well as a nationally known member of the movements for social and Church reform. For forty years from 1827, moreover, the diocese was under the careful guidance of a famous Evangelical bishop, Richard Charles Sumner, the first Bishop of Winchester since the Reformation to be installed in person in his own cathedral. Perhaps the most famous of Hampshire church reforms effected in Sumner's time was the drawing up of a proper scheme for the administration of St. Cross Hospital.

These early Victorian Hampshire people, Buckinghams, Barings, Heathcotes, Bonham-Carters, Kebles, Kingsleys, were conscious of social distinctions, but they all believed that a true religious belief combined with a suitable education was the greatest potential remedy for the social evils of their times. A number of Hampshire villages claimed to have model schools usually supported by the local Anglican church or Dissenting chapel. In the towns, Mechanics Institutes provided all kinds of classes and lectures for working men. The county was already well endowed with grammar schools, and after the Education Act of 1871 primary (Board) schools were set up in every district not already covered by voluntary effort. The provision of schools and the administration of education is now one of the most important tasks of the County Council, for it is that authority, set up by Act of Parliament in 1889, which today bears the main burden of public life in Hampshire.

Further reading: *Sir William Heathcote, Bart*, F. Awdry (Wykeham Press, 1905).
In a Liberal Tradition, V. Bonham-Carter (Constable, 1960).
Rural Rides, William Cobbett, ed. G. D. H. and M. Cole (Davies, 1930).
The Tichborne Claimant, Douglas Woodruff (Hollis & Carter, 1957).
Enter Rumour, R. B. Martin, (Faber & Faber, 1962). (The best and most recent account of the St. Cross Scandal).
Dulce Domum, C. A. E. Moberley (Murray, 1911).
William Cobbett, W. Baring Pemberton (Penguin, 1949).
The Dust of Combat (A life of Charles Kingsley), R. B. Martin (Faber & Faber, 1959).

XVIII

Some Recent Changes

THE year 1889 marks an important stage in the development of local government in Hampshire for in that year the first elections took place for membership of the new County Council. Most of the members elected in fact proved to be already County Magistrates, who carried on the work of local government in much the same way as they had done before the Act. Today, the administrative area of the county includes the whole of Hampshire, except for the Isle of Wight, the county of the town of Southampton, and the more recent county boroughs of Portsmouth and Bournemouth. Within the area of the county administration there are nine municipal boroughs, the majority of which are ancient chartered towns, six urban districts and some two hundred and four parish councils. All these bodies are made up of elected members, members elected freely by ballot at regular intervals, by electors who are over the age of twenty-one and who are normally resident in the locality of the election. It is the reform of local government which has proved to be one of the greatest changes Hampshire has seen in the last hundred years.

Another area which has changed is that of the diocese. The bishopric of Winchester has been greatly diminished by the creation of the new see of Guildford in Surrey in 1927 to the north, and by a similar diminution in the south in the same year, in this case within the county, by the creation of the new diocese of Portsmouth with its cathedral in the old parish church there. The diocese now consists of most of Hampshire and the Channel Islands, annexed to it in 1568. The greatest ecclesiastical change from the mid-nineteenth century onwards was, however, the creation of a vast number of new parishes. By 1918, nearly half the parishes in the diocese had been created in the previous

hundred years, chiefly because of the growth of new areas, and the development of older towns. In that year, Bournemouth alone had fourteen parishes, there were nineteen new parishes at Portsmouth and Southsea, sixteen in Southampton, as well as those in Aldershot and Eastleigh, and the parishes created on what had been waste land near Botley each with what has been called a strawberry church, since it was market gardening and the growing of strawberries which accounted for the rise in the population of the area. Reform within the Church, and particularly the Oxford Movement was a reason for the formation of new parishes at Ampfield, Colden Common and East Boldre. This attempt to build churches in new areas of population is a conscious policy in the diocese today.

It is perhaps the pressure of population and of population movements, combined with industrial changes, which most affected Hampshire in the last fifty years. The New Forest, though it still produces much good timber, no longer provides the essential materials of the Royal Navy, whose new ships are rarely built in the south of England, ships whose construction depends on the heavy products of iron and steel, not Hampshire-centred industries. Their maintenance and re-fitting at Portsmouth, however, has encouraged the growth of heavy industry there, and at Southampton likewise the merchant navy needs similar services. Heavy industrial development has become an essential function of the economies of Southampton and Portsmouth, and the Hampshire coastline has also been altered by the needs of the internal combustion engine, particularly by the construction of a huge oil refinery on Southampton Water conveniently placed for the reception of crude oil from the distant corners of the world. Side by side with this industrial change has come a great increase in the tourist industry, in the appreciation of the New Forest as a holiday resort, the growth of Bournemouth and of Southsea near Portsmouth as sea-side towns, and of the Isle of Wight where Queen Victoria's long continued use of Osborne helped to make the Island a fashionable resort, as did Tennyson's love of his home at Farringford in Freshwater. The Isle of Wight's railway system, which did so much to open up the Island to visitors, has been partially closed down in recent years, except for lines between Ryde, Cowes and Ventnor.

On the mainland, too, the coming of the railways has been followed by the closing of many branch lines and the demolition of stations and bridges. It is the problem of ever-increasing road traffic which has become most serious, with all that this increase means in the provision of car parks in ancient towns and of fast new roads cutting through the countryside. There can be little doubt that the appearance of Hampshire is changing rapidly, and much of the old variation of both county and town is being obliterated by repetitive building, stereotyped shop fronts and unnecessary urban sprawl. Yet the land still retains its inherent and distinctive characteristics, wherein each individual, whether the county is his by birth or adoption, sees a Hampshire made by the movement of peoples and by the hand of history.

Index

INDEX